D0317968

REMEMBERING
THE HIGH STREET

REMEMBERING
THE HIGH STREET
A Nostalgic Look at Famous Names

Gordon Thorburn

First published in Great Britain in 2011 by
Remember When
an imprint of
Pen & Sword Books Ltd
47 Church Street
Barnsley
South Yorkshire
S70 2AS

Copyright © Gordon Thorburn, 2011

ISBN: 978-1-84468-098-6

The right of Gordon Thorburn to be identified as Author of this
Work has been asserted by him in accordance with the Copyright,
Designs and Patents Act 1988.

A CIP catalogue record for this book is
available from the British Library.

All rights reserved. No part of this book may be reproduced or
transmitted in any form or by any means, electronic or mechanical
including photocopying, recording or by any information storage and
retrieval system, without permission from the Publisher in writing.

Typeset in 11/13pt Palatino by
Concept, Huddersfield, West Yorkshire

Printed and bound by
CPI Group (UK) Ltd, Croydon, CR0 4YY

Pen & Sword Books Ltd incorporates the Imprints of Pen & Sword
Aviation, Pen & Sword Family History, Pen & Sword Maritime, Pen &
Sword Military, Pen & Sword Discovery, Wharncliffe Local History,
Wharncliffe True Crime, Wharncliffe Transport, Pen & Sword Select, Pen
& Sword Military Classics, Leo Cooper, The Praetorian Press, Remember
When, Seaforth Publishing and Frontline Publishing.

For a complete list of Pen & Sword titles please contact
PEN & SWORD BOOKS LIMITED
47 Church Street, Barnsley, South Yorkshire, S70 2AS, England
E-mail: enquiries@pen-and-sword.co.uk
Website: www.pen-and-sword.co.uk

Contents

Worcester Park, between Epsom, Sutton and Kingston, in the 1940s and West Byfleet in the 1960s (see top, next page) seem to illustrate Nystrom's point, although Barnet high street in 1962 (see bottom, next page), when it was still the A1 Great North Road, shows the opposite – almost nothing but the chains, with Boots, Woolies, Burton's, MacFisheries and Dewhurst all featuring.

Chains have enjoyed the most rapid development since 1920, but in recent years even they show indications of having reached their maturity of relative growth. The single, independently owned stores, while hardest hit by competition of the newer types of retailing, are now apparently holding their own. There are now more of such stores than ever before.

P H Nystrom,
Elements of Retail Selling, 1936.

A seaside W H Smith's, in Prestatyn, 1922. Note the early postcard spinner and the wooden spades for the beach. Newspapers and books sent to any part of the world, bookbinding from a single volume to a whole library executed in all styles, advertisements placed in London, provincial and foreign papers.

The way we were in 1957 – opening day, W H Smith, Swansea.

Acknowledgements

Many thanks are due to: Hilary Hyde, Curator, W H Smith Museum; for some of the advertisements, www.historyworld.co.uk; Susan Butler and members of the Goole WEA History Group, see www. btinternet.com/~susanebutler/; and to Colin French, creator and curator of www.macfisheries.co.uk.

Introduction

There used to be butcher, baker, grocer, greengrocer, draper, Boots, ironmonger, pub, W H Smith, cafe, bank, shoe shop, jeweller, Marks and Spencer, furniture shop, hotel, second-hand book-seller, off licence, haberdasher, Woolworth's, confectioner, cobbler, tobacconist, electrical showroom, Burton's, gas showroom, ladies' fashions, Home & Colonial, gentlemen's outfitters, and more, and maybe a department store, and several versions of some. What do we have now?

Pound shop, charity shop, building society branch, ladies' hairdresser, betting shop, coffee shop, charity shop, shop boarded up, building society branch, sandwich shop, shop boarded up, kebab takeaway, charity shop, ladies' hairdresser, card shop, Indian takeaway, mobile phone shop – we exaggerate but make the point. So what has gone wrong – if it is wrong?

There is no single force to account for this change. Supermarkets must be a contributor, in or out of town. Out-of-town shopping centres, or retail parks, or malls, or outlet villages, whatever you want to call them, must be another. Greedy landlords pushing rents ever higher, business rates, complacent and/or blind councils under-investing, the internet, chain stores that are run from far away and pull out when targets are missed, lack of foresight by just about everybody, property developers who demolish willy-nilly and erect monsters, planning committees who give permission to the developers – it's all far too much for the butcher and the baker to resist.

Why is the kitchen so clean.?

Why is the joint so juicy ?

Why are her cakes so evenly baked ?

And why is she saving money ?

Because her cooker's electric ! *

*An electric cooker gives the exact heat wanted, exactly where it's wanted. It cooks evenly— always. And it's wonderfully cheap to run.

See the latest timer-controlled electric cookers at your Eastern Electricity Service Centre

ELECTRICITY

29-56

The Electricity Act of 1947 and the Gas Act of 1948 nationalised those industries and electricity- and gas-board showrooms began appearing on every high street, even in small towns, where before they did not exist at all. The twelve regional gas boards, for instance, replaced over 1,000 individual gas companies, some privately run, some run by the local council. There was a similar shake-up in electricity, as when the East Dereham Urban District Council's electrical efforts were joined with those of the Frinton-on-Sea Electric Light and Power Company, and about forty others, to form the Eastern Electricity Board, who thought it wise in 1956 to publish this advertisement.

The showrooms, where people paid their bills as well as buying their cookers and fires, began to disappear after the power industries were privatised by the Acts of 1989. Some were sold as going concerns into private hands, some just went. Similar stores now remaining generally sell everything, gas and electric, and woodburning stoves too.

Newton Abbot, Devon, in the 1920s, has a soda fountain – the very latest thing, as seen in the Hollywood moving and talking pictures – in a building dated 1690. Someone on a bicycle has gone into the stationers, and a policeman directs the traffic or, more accurately, waits for some traffic to direct. Now, that's what you call a high street.

In the UK today, most chain retailers see too many problems in setting up or expanding on the average high street. Old and legally intertwined freeholds and leases are hard to unravel, and the big names are better off in purpose-built shopping centres rather than the organically-grown mish-mash of the old towns. They don't want to be in so many towns either. About 300 seems the optimum these days.

Some would say, so what? Who cares, when you can go online, or get in the car and do the whole thing in one hit? Who wants to walk down high streets in the wind and rain, looking in windows, going in and out of different shops, when you can see it all at home on a screen, or park your car a trolley-push away from all those different shops amalgamated under one roof?

Many would say, it's cheaper, the modern way. Such an opinion is impossible to prove. Nobody can say how much things would cost now if there were no supermarkets and no internet. Almost all would agree that it's more convenient, less of a bother, but convenience and good quality – all kinds of quality – do not necessarily go together.

In any case, and whatever the opinion, there can be no doubt that our high streets and market squares are in danger of becoming ghosts of shopping past, and some are there already. The councils of a few large cities are reporting a quarter of their shop premises lying empty.

Billingham, County Durham (above), and Bolton, Lancashire in the 1960s (opposite) already had modern high streets, or 'developments'. These were built on the reasonable assumption that main shopping streets would always be a central feature of our towns. Sometimes, such developments involved the destruction of what had been before, which became a matter of regret when, forty years on, the 'new' high streets began to suffer closures from the Supermarket Effect just the same as the old ones.

Some town councils in wealthy areas have no fears. Where there was a butcher's shop, now there is an antiques shop. Where there was a greengrocer's, there's an art gallery. Where there was an ironmonger's, there's an interior designer's.

For the rest, well, it looks like a downward spiral. Optimists may try to make a go of keeping a shop but, like would-be restaurateurs, they mostly fail. The banks won't lend like they used to, and who can blame them? They're probably doing their customers a favour.

Common sense says that the great majority of shoppers have a finite amount of money, so they will not spend more in the high street on top of what they spend in the supermarket and the mall. So, either they are persuaded to switch allegiances, which is unlikely, or the high street must offer something better and/or different. Otherwise, it will all be boarded up except for Boots, Oxfam and the kebab place.

Still, as we cry into our glasses of half-price Tesco Argentinean red, and munch our Waitrose party-size spring rolls while waiting for the Sainsbury's chicken rogan josh to heat up, we can at least remember how things used to be, and console ourselves with the one great eternal truth: the older we get, the better it was.

CHAPTER 1

How the first-ever shop led to M&S

The first-ever shop had no staff, no till, no shelves, although it might have had a kind of trolley. Representatives of Tribe A, who were hunters and had a surplus of game at the moment, went to the accustomed spot with their bag and laid it out on the ground. They gave a call, or blew a horn, to advertise their wares, then retired to a safe distance.

Representatives of Tribe B, who were farmers and metal workers, summoned by the call, came forward to inspect the goods on offer, with no interference from sales people or other gobby types. Tribe B had brought with them some sacks of grain, some arrow-heads and a few spears. Judging what they believed to be the value of the meat lying there, and trying to restrain their salivating imaginations from a feast of roast wild boar and barbecued dodo, they placed on the ground their consideration of price, in grain and sharp metal, and retired behind some suitable trees.

The men of Tribe A came forth and looked at the offer. One fellow was for accepting it, another thought it a bleeding liberty, two more thought it was almost but not quite. They picked up one dodo and retired. The men of B, knowing what their wives would say if they didn't bring home all the bacon, stepped forward, put a couple more arrow-heads down, and went behind their trees.

The A team added the dodo again, with an extra squirrel as a mark of good faith, gathered up the corn and the weaponry, and disappeared into the undergrowth. The B men went back to a delighted village and all dined happily ever after. This very formal kind of shopping, called 'silent trade' or 'dumb barter', was practised until fairly recently in uncivilised parts and may still be.

Closer contact between traders may result in even greater formality. The Maoris, for instance, had a system of trade not unlike our exchange of presents at Christmas. We want to be lavish with our giving and often go beyond what we can really afford, so that Brownie points may be accumulated. There is always the danger that we as recipients may not see our new scarf as quite the *quid pro quo* for the diamond brooch or the half dozen of Lafite, but never mind. It is better to give than to receive. The same quandary was often encountered by the Maoris, who would compete for generous reputation in their giving but still needed to keep the exchange of fish for vegetables in line with the household budget.

Meanwhile, in other societies, the goal was gain, not prestige through munificence, and so the best hagglers and shrewdest deal-makers were the ones who grew rich according to local criteria and got their prestige that way. You could also find a kind of two-tier tradition in shopping, where the bargaining for certain high classes of goods was conducted formally and ceremonially, while that for life's necessities was the usual rude scrabble for advantage.

Such scrabbling led naturally to forms of currency. While value might be set on strings of beads, quantities of salt or red feathers and hooli-hooli skirts, these were not true currencies unless all other goods could be valued in their terms and all in a society recognised them as having that value. You want a cow? That'll be twenty strings of beads. You want a pint of milk? Two blue beads and a yellow, please.

In Europe, lumps of metal became a sort of money, valued according to weight. The pound, *libra pondo*, a certain weight of bronze, became the Roman standard in early days, and it was but a short step from lugging masses of bronze about to the idea of much smaller and more convenient pieces of rarer metals, authorised as genuine by the Emperor's head depicted thereon. The gold *solidus*, Latin for whole, true or entire, became the definitive Roman coin, at first divided into twenty-five *denarii* and later twelve.

As is the way of things, money and prices went in opposite directions over the years, and Charlemagne (742–814) had to abandon the gold standard, settling instead for 240 *denarii* cut from a pound weight of silver, an idea he may have copied from King Offa of Mercia, as central England was then known, who had silver pennies circulating by 760. There was no pound coin, obviously, it being too heavy for any purse, and no shilling or *solidus* either, but these terms were used in accounting. And the rest, as Offa or Charlemagne might have predicted, was pure Libra, Solidus, Denarius, until some idiot turned it all into pees.

Mercor, mercatus, mercari

The Latin verb to trade, deal in, buy, from which in English we get market and merchant, is one of the evolutionary verbal strands that has led to our high streets and market squares. *Sceoppa*, Anglo-Saxon, a booth, a lean-to, related to *scipen*, a cattle shed (shippon), gives us the other strand.

The original shop (or *sceoppa*) was a workshop. In Saxon times, all consumer goods were hand-made by individual craftsmen, so the potter threw his pots in his lean-to and the smith had the same set-up in his booth.

Later, in more luxurious times, when trades had developed to suit the requirements of the moderately wealthy town dweller, if you wanted a pair of gloves, a hat, a pair of shoes, a cooking pot, a nice doublet and hose for your daughter's wedding, you went to the glover's or the shoemaker's or the tailor's house, where he had his place of work. If he was very good at his craft and therefore had a secure and busy trade, he would also have a space where he might show some things he had made earlier. These might be for sale, or to show patterns and skills, or both.

'Shop' can still mean place of work today, for instance in a factory that has specialised departments such as a machine shop or a paint shop. When we talk shop, it's only about British Home Stores or Asda if we happen to work there. In some parts of the country, where the local dialect is nearer the original Viking/Saxon than it is in the BBC, shop can also mean place of residence. Even so, by and large we mean a retailing store when we say shop, which in turn means that the space the craftsman allowed for showing his work has taken over entirely.

Of course there were other ways of buying pots and hats. A pedlar might come to your door. For manufactured goods as opposed to food and everyday consumables, you could go to the annual or twice-yearly fair. Fairs were markets on the grand scale. You knew when they would occur, you knew what would be for sale, and you made every effort to get there.

Markets, by definition places where buyers and sellers assembled, knowing that each other would be there at a certain time, were more frequent and more local. The woman with the eggs, the farmer with his meat or his vegetables, didn't want to travel far nor, indeed, could afford to take more than a day off production work to go to market, sell the produce and buy whatever was needed from the other stall-holders.

This was all very well as a system for rural and small-town Britain. Large-town Britain wanted markets every day except Sunday. As the population increased and business thrived in urban centres, selling had to become a trade of its own and the place of sale had to become permanent.

It's worth looking at the birth and growth of these urban centres. We'll use Leeds as an example, not because it's unique or even unusual, but because it's typical. The same sorts of things that happened in Leeds, hub of a mighty cloth-producing region, happened in Birmingham (metal-bashing), Newcastle (coal and ships), Liverpool (sea trade), Sheffield (more metal-bashing), Manchester (more cloth) and all the rest of the industrial giants that started as nothing special but became convenient for wealth production.

The Venerable Bede mentioned Leeds (Loidis) in passing, in his *History of the English Church and People* c. 730AD, but the first hard evidence of what it was like in early days is in the *Domesday Book*, 1086. Leeds (Ledes by then) was an unremarkable agricultural settlement, important above its station because of the ford across the River Aire where the bridge (or brig) at the bottom of Briggate now is. The Domesday scribes recorded ten carucates, six bovates of land suitable for royal taxing (eight bovates in a carucate, as eny fule kno, altogether roughly 1,000 acres or 400 hectares), held by twenty-seven villeins, four sokemen and four bordars. These were peasants of several ranks, the bordar being the lowest of the low, all subservient to the lord of the manor as his tenants and all rendering service to him in payment for the use of his bovates.

There was also a church with a priest, a water mill, and some meadowland. The whole lot of Leeds in 1086 was deemed to be worth £7 a year. This is an amount of revenue almost impossible to evaluate in modern terms. Something like £100,000 would not be far out, or very approximately £100 of our money per acre, which goes to show how productive you were when farming with ox-hauled ploughs and sowing and reaping by hand.

No mention of cloth-making then, but by the 1300s there was a bridge over the ford and cloth merchants were displaying their wares on it. Leeds was on the up, and by 1560 the heart of the modern city was beginning to show, with Briggate the primary street, Kirkgate below and Upper and Lower Head Row above and heading off for York, and a narrow lane where Vicar Lane now is. There was a second river in the open then, variously called Adel Beck and Sheepscar Beck, flowing more or less where Sheepscar Street runs today.

In 1725, Daniel Defoe found a 'large, wealthy and prosperous town', and a Portuguese visitor around the same time much admired the shops and the quantity and variety of food coming in. An American visitor in 1777 saw that Leeds had 'many well-filled shops, and various trades; its principal business in narrow and coarse woollen cloths, consigned to foreign orders'. Weavers would bring their weekly output to the cloth market, later the purpose-built cloth hall, where they'd sell to merchants and other middlemen.

At the start of the nineteenth century, when the population of Leeds was around the 20,000 mark, there was a market each week for livestock and another for wheat, barley and oats. Food and general provisions were sold twice a week, as was cloth. Only fifty years later, with a population grown three or four times, the business folk of Leeds had transformed everything. The provisions market was off the street and into a market hall, as were meat and fish, and there was a special building for general goods. Corn was bought and sold in a corn exchange, and trade in securities had been brought out of the coffee houses into a stock exchange.

Charles Dickens didn't like it, though. Some eighty years after that American, and despite a comfortable night at the boarding-house which is now the Scarbrough pub, he thought Leeds 'an odious place'. He was offended by the chimneys that marked the scores of woollen mills and the three dozen flax mills.

In Defoe's time the population had been about 15,000; by 1861 there were that many in Irish immigrants alone, then the Russian Jews came and, by the start of the First World War, Leeds was approaching half a million people.

Got safe to Leeds took an Omnibus which carried us to an Inn. Here we stopt till Monday. Leeds is a fine town, but very dirty and dusty, and so was the Inn. It was markett day, we could see the stalls out of our window, as we drove along in the Omnibus, I saw a great number of shoestalls; I concluded it was of no use to count them, for they increased as we went. I think there was not so much earthenware as at Hull, one stall before the Inn had oranges and lemons to sell. I went out and bought two oranges for sixpence: they were fine large ones.

The young author of this diary entry, Sarah Ellis, travelled from Hull to Selby by boat, and from Selby to Leeds by railway (her first time), in 1815. The picture was taken soon after Lewis's opened in the Headrow in 1932.

In the evening went with Mrs. S. and E. to see a Bazzaar; it was like going into a large hall fill'd with shops, some for toys, some with caps and collars etc., some with jewelry, and various things besides. We walk'd round the bottom part, then ascended the stairs, which was in like manner occupied; one person had a very long shop. I thought she must look sharp when she was at one end, that she was not rob'd at the other. I purchased a pair of chamber Bellows here, as I wishd for something to remember Leeds. It was getting so dusky I was troubled to see. Mrs. S. made some little purchase, I think a pair of salts; we then return'd to the Inn, and found the markett which we had to pass thro – very busy.

Around Dickens's time and later, a massive change happened in our cities. The higgledy-piggledy, as-and-when maze of dwellings and alleyways of the typical city centre was being cleared and replaced by broad streets and factories, banks, warehouses, offices and shops. In Leeds, you could walk along Boar Lane or Briggate and see all kinds of wares for sale, displayed with every incentive to buy, behind large plate-glass windows. Messrs Pullan had their 'Central Shawl and Mantle Warehouse' on the corner (mantle as in cloak, not mantle as in gas), next to Bissington's shoe shop. Elsewhere Mr Whitehouse would repair your watch, Bostock's the chemist would supply your medicinal requirements, as would Taylor's.

In Bradford in 1843 a petition in favour of incorporation as a borough was signed by, among many others, 2,100 shopkeepers, and the petition against by 1,003, but there was no thought yet, there or in Leeds, of a Schofield's, or a Lewis's, nor any other department store, and no thought either of a penny bazaar, run by a Lithuanian called Michael Marks, or a tiny herbalist/chemist's shop, run by a Nottinghamshire farmer's son called Jesse Boot, turning into a glamorous store on every high street in every large town in the country. The first hint of what was to come could be observed by the far-sighted in the expansion of a certain book-seller, newsagent and stationer, galloping along beside the railways: W H Smith.

The Greeks and Romans had shops. Often, they were part of what we would now call a development. A new public building, or even a grand private residence, would incorporate small shops open to the street (we might call them units), the rent from which would defray public expenditure or enrich the private resident in question. Many of our own high street shops came about in the same way.

A stroll past The Grove Hotel and into Spring Gardens in Buxton in the 1880s would have revealed a number of integral units, built to a standard design but occupied variously by C Adams, Practical Boot and Shoe Maker; H Newbold, Draper, Hosier, Mercer and Glover; J Shelmerdine, Fruiterer Etc; E Glauert, Watchmaker and Jeweller; Tomlinson Bromley & Co., Chemists; E White, Tobacconist, Wholesale and Retail Cigar Merchant; Trehearn & Hallifield, Stationers & Newsagents, and so on and so on. In 1863, as part of his strategy of constant improvement to Buxton's facilities as a spa resort, the Duke of Devonshire built the Hot Baths Colonnade, a row of eight shops, all with planning permission.

The great Buxton building boom occurred over a relatively short time, fuelled by the Victorians' love of spas, and a quick whizz through the town leaves one with the impression of an architectural unity, massively expressed in stone. Sidmouth, south-east Devon, evolved more gently and over a longer time, from fishing village to holiday resort, which may explain why a walk along Fore Street and the rest of the town centre in Victorian years would have had something in common with a similar walk now. Henry Bartlett, Fresh Fish Daily, has disappeared from Church Street, and J Spencer no longer offers donkey carts and bath chairs for hire, while Culverwell's stationers and fancy goods lives on only in memory and in *The Sidmouth Herald*. Lake's Seed and Canine Stores is gone, and Tedbury's butcher's, and Veale's wine merchant's, and A C Drewe, Purveyor of English Meat. There's a Tesco convenience store at the top of the high street that was a newsagent, a Co-op in the middle, a Lidl and a Waitrose on the outskirts, but Hayman's butcher's is still there, and Skinner's dairy, Potbury's furniture store, and John Field's little draper's shop is twenty times the size as the famous department store.

In the late 1800s, department stores and chains of specialised stores followed the lead of W H Smith, enabled by the novelty of a national transport system of railways and better roads. Such things had not been possible earlier, at any rate. The business just wasn't there. In 1800, there was nowhere in Britain, outside London, with

Looking from the market place up Old Fore Street in Sidmouth, around 1960, the view is very similar to today's, except the street has been pedestrianised. The shop names are all different but the buildings are still there, that's the important thing. The organic growth over centuries has not been wrecked for a charmless, brutal 'development'.

a population of 100,000, but in the ten years from 1821, Manchester, Birmingham, Leeds, Liverpool, Bradford and Sheffield all grew by an average of 50 per cent. By 1891 there were twenty-three places in England and Wales with populations over 100,000, and over 30 per cent of all our people lived in them and the capital. Almost 20 per cent of Scots lived in Glasgow.

The high street as we know it and think of it had been transformed from a residential street with some local shops and businesses into a street entirely lined by shops and businesses, some of them branches of large chains and corporations with headquarters elsewhere. Although every town would soon have a Burton and a Boots, local names predominated and a lot of shops had apartments above.

On the one hand, bearing in mind the changes we have seen recently, and on the other the earlier appearance of some chain stores such as W H Smith and Hepworth's Tailors, we have to conclude that the high street of blessed memory really only lasted half a century, let us say from the end of the First World War to the early 1970s. By then, the first Arndale Centres had been built

(Jarrow, Bradford, Wandsworth), charity shops were becoming common, building societies were amalgamating and thinking they might like to open scores of new branches, and planning permission had been granted to those who wished to rip out the heart of old Manchester and replace it with one enormous brick outhouse.

Department story

The idea behind the department store is not dissimilar to that behind the supermarket: sell lots of different things under one roof and people will rejoice at not having to troll around the streets looking for stuff, and the shop owners will be able to make economies of scale on overheads. Supermarkets began, and mainly remain, as places to buy everyday necessities, while department stores have always dealt largely in goods we only buy from time to time, such as clothes, furniture, the perfumes of Araby, jewellery and the like.

The department store's competitors are therefore the individual tailor's shop or jeweller, whether that is one of a chain or a local trader, just as the supermarket's competitors are, or rather were in most cases, the individual butcher, grocer and greengrocer. There would appear to be sense in both ideas and room for both in the great scheme of things, yet individual department stores have disappeared from the majority of our high streets. The exceptions are the biggest hitters in London and a few noble names out in the sticks, such as Field's of Sidmouth, Fenwick's of Newcastle, Jarrold's of Norwich, Hill's of Spalding, Bentall's of Kingston, Bradbeer's in Hampshire, Wroe's in Cornwall, Aitken and Niven of Edinburgh, Wetherell's of Selby, and more, but nothing like so many as there used to be.

Their recent difficulties have lain chiefly in two areas: costs and staff. Their premises tend to be in town centres, and by their nature large and rambling, all of which makes them expensive to run. It is not uncommon for the operating costs of a department store to be well over a third of turnover, unlike supermarkets, which are much more efficient for all sorts of reasons. Also, supermarkets do not rely on sales staff, beyond a shelf-filler knowing where the water chestnuts are, while department stores rely on them almost entirely for successful trading. Unlike the local dress shop, where the same people tend to be there to serve year after year, customers don't often get to know department store sales people. Relationships are not built up so much, therefore sales staff have to be even better at their job.

Be that as it may, the idea was a good one at the time. The first department store in Britain is usually claimed to be Whiteley's, developed from a small draper's shop in Westbourne Grove, London, opened by William Whiteley (qv) in 1863. In fact, the credit probably goes to a chap called Emmerson Bainbridge who ran a similar business in Newcastle upon Tyne and began keeping his accounts by department in 1849. Lewis's (not John Lewis, qv) started in Liverpool in 1856, expanded into most of the major northern cities, shrank again back to Liverpool, went into receivership in 2007 and was bought as a going concern. Bainbridge's sold out to John Lewis in 1952.

The oldest independent department store still going in the world has to be Austin's of Derry, with trading origins going back to 1830, although many authorities, including Encyclopaedia Britannica, give the credit for inventing the notion to the French, with Bon Marché starting out in the usual way as a small draper's shop. That may not have been until 1838, but it is not disputed that the new building in 1852 was the first designed specifically for the purpose of a department store.

In the early/mid-nineteenth century, department stores were opened in Dublin, New York, Sydney and elsewhere, mostly by flamboyant characters who understood marketing very well, and how to exploit their staff. By 1867, Whiteley had a row of shops, some of which had several departments, and by the 1880s he had eighteen adjoining shops. Fires, possibly arson attacks, resulted in a vast new building in Queensway, which allowed the successors of 'The Universal Provider', as he billed himself, to claim the largest shop in the country.

The man was dead (1907) by then but his ego lived on in the store's theatre and rooftop golf course, and how pleased he would have been to be mentioned by G B Shaw in *Pygmalion*. Gordon Selfridge (qv) bought the business in 1927 and it went through various hands after the war, ending up bust in 1981. Rebuilt over the next few years, it opened as a shopping centre in 1989. This is a fate befalling a number of department stores. In particular, your correspondent thinks of the elegant building of Rowntree's, dominating upper Westborough in Scarborough, sold to Debenham's, demolished and replaced with the most hideous, featureless pile of red bricks anyone could imagine, housing a shopping centre which, we could say, is no more than a department store rearranged.

Talking of Scarborough, that was a town with three department stores. Your *hoi polloi* went to Boyes's in Queen Street, by the market, which is the original Boyes of a chain now of thirty-six stores in the north and east Midlands of England. William Boyes began in 1881 with cloth leftovers in his father's grocer's shop at 26 Eastborough. His much-expanded Queen Street premises he called The Remnant Warehouse, and that's the sort of reputation the firm built, kind of cheap and cheerful. He's listed in 1890 as general and fancy draper, remnant and job stuff dealer.

Meanwhile, the great middle section of society went to Rowntree's and later to Marks & Spencer, but the Scarborough glitterati went to that other M&S, Marshall and Snelgrove, the store near the town hall, more or less opposite Greensmith and Thackwray, Indian & Colonial Outfitters. This is where Modom shopped for her mink, and silks and satins, and her wedding outfit. Actually, from 1919 onwards she was going to Debenham's, but never mind.

John Snelgrove went into partnership with James Marshall in 1848, and in 1851 began building a ladies' fashions store in Oxford Street. Going in completely the opposite direction to some of our other heroes, such as Burton, Woolworth and Boot, these two set out to be exclusive. They did sell ready-to-wear but made in their own workrooms, and Modom could always consult the staff in the couturier department if in any doubt.

James Marshall junior took over the business and expanded mainly in the north and Midlands, following the money in the big cities but also in places like Harrogate and Southport and, of course, Scarborough.

Mrs Pankhurst smashed the windows of the Oxford Street shop in 1912. Came the war and business fell away. In 1919, struggling, the firm merged with Debenham and Freebody but kept the name. Virginia Woolf mentions it in *Orlando* but high points from then on are difficult to detect, although customers in the Birmingham shop in 1960 would have seen clothes modelled by Mandy Rice-Davies.

Harmony

This new Roussel creation gives perfect shape and uplift to the bust . . . moulding the figure in smooth harmonious lines.

Booklet A.71 with details of all Roussel models is now available on request.

VAGUE SOUVENIR and JASMIN — Two intriguing Guerlain perfumes direct from Paris. At all Roussel branches.

J. Roussel Ltd
(Paris · London)

17a St. Ann St., Manchester
Phone: Deansgate 8005

84 Bold St., Liverpool
Phone: Royal 7784

179-181 Regent St. & 137 New Bond St., London
and at Aberdeen, Birmingham, Bristol, Glasgow, Leeds

Roussel's department stores, once of Manchester, Liverpool, London, Paris and elsewhere, are no more. One of their London stores, in Regent Street, is now Viyella. The other, in New Bond Street, is YSL Rive Gauche. In Liverpool it's become Madame Foners/ Liaison Lingerie, which is appropriate enough if a little on the warm side.

29

There was no real ladies' chain store equivalent to Burton, John Collier, Hepworth and the like. Richard Shops and similar firms never had the universality of the men's tailors, possibly because they were run by men who thought that women would be too difficult to please. There are such chains now, of course, but back in the 1950s, before that and well after that, ordinary women mainly went to department stores (maybe not Roussel in this case) or the local drapers and dress shops. The two ladies are pictured in Whitby in 1954. What can we say?

In 1973 those stores still open became Debenham's by name as well as ownership.

If she couldn't see just what she wanted in Marshall's and Modom was a stranger in Scarborough, she could stroll past Boots Corner and go walkabout. She might note one or more of J Sinfield's seven tobacconist's shops, and the Balmoral Hotel. Further up the town she would see Marks & Spencer, J Tonks and Son furniture shop, Harding's bookshop, The Pavilion Hotel with its Vaults pub, James Beale men's outfitters, Timothy White's and Taylor's, Mann & Co. stockbrokers, Cook Fowler & Outhet solicitors, the Co-op in Unity House, Kisby's tobacconist, H O Taylor stationer's, W H Smith, Leader's ladies' clothes, Bradshaw's opticians, the Londesborough cinema, Woodhead's baker's, Good's electrical shop, and many others.

Perhaps she'd find her heart's desire in Rowntree's, a store run by a fairly eminent family, including Joshua Rowntree, Liberal Member of Parliament, John Rowntree and Sons, grocers and provision merchants, but more importantly Wm Rowntree and Sons, drapers, hatters, hosiers, cabinet-makers, house furnishers. They were also undertakers. As we said earlier, department stores tended to sell what we only want occasionally.

CHAPTER 2

Once upon a time in Goole

The population of this east Yorkshire port at the time of our survey in 1937 was approximately 19,500, which was about 2,000 more than it is now. The population in ancient times would have been verging on nil, with possibly a few peasant farmers scratching a living in the marshes.

There are several reasons for the town's existence, none of them really natural. It stands at the confluence of the rivers Don and Ouse, but that was only after the Don was diverted in the time of King Charles I, which made it ideal for exporting south Yorkshire coal. It is the last bridging possibility for the Ouse before that river widens into the Humber, so it would have been handy for going through on the way to somewhere else if there hadn't been more useful bridges upstream.

Mainly, there was the construction of the Knottingley canal by the Aire and Calder Navigation Co., opened in 1826, which pre-supposed Goole as the port for goods coming and going and, in effect, as a company town, or village since it had only about 450 folk at the start.

In 1937, the main exports were coal and other raw materials plus clothing, pottery and machinery. Imports included some heavy goods but also food and oil. The LNER dropped passengers off for steamship services to the Continent. It was a busy place and the right size to attract quite a few of the chains to open shops there and, like all towns and cities then, it had many, many small and medium-sized retail businesses owned and run by the locals. These really were local shops for local people, and there was plenty for you there.

Let us take a walk down the chief shopping street of Goole, Boothferry Road, now pedestrianised but in 1937 nobody had thought of such a thing for a main thoroughfare. Boothferry Road was previously Murham Avenue and a desirable residential area for those families not happy with the idea of living among the working people in the company town. Gradually it became that marvellous thing, the typical high street.

We shall start at the top end, on the even-numbered side, heading towards the market square, so that we can take a break in the George IV Inn before returning up the odd-numbered side.

The first three shops were small lock-ups – a greengrocer, a barber and a tobacconist. Next door to the smokes were the sweets, where Mrs Scutt kept a confectioner's shop at number 132, followed by Dewing the chemist and optician, Eccles and Co. the drapers, and the first of many butchers, Herbert Needham.

There was a tea merchant, Altham and Co., next to a fish and chip shop, another confectioner, and the first of the bigger places, Northern Clothing, where the parents of pupils at Goole Grammar bought their offspring's uniforms. This was a Hull firm with several branches, all now gone.

Geoff LeVoguer was there in the 1950s. 'I remember the Northern Clothing Co. shop on Boothferry Road. It faced the old St John's Hospital opposite. Also The Cosy Carlton Picture House, run by Mr Austin, ably assisted, among others, by one Billy King. It had a well-stocked sweet shop annexed to it.'

The double frontage after Northern Clothing belonged to the drapery and shoe departments of the Goole Co-operative Society (see page 134 for the Co-op's history), and next door to that was Hopley's fruiterer's. A hosiery shop, a butcher, a grocer, another draper, another grocer, another draper, Fleming's furniture store, Emsley's chemist's, and a well-known name in Goole, T Sheppard and Co., musical instrument warehouse.

Frank Philpott writes: 'I remember my mother drawing her Co-op divi once a year. You had to save all your receipts. My brother and I were outfitted for school at the Northern Clothing Co. every year. Stores I remember … Crapper's the butcher … Sheppard's for records … Curry's for bicycles. Home & Colonial.

The early owners of the butcher's business at numbers 78 and 80 were a German family, the Strickers, but the First World War, anti-German feeling and internment put an end to that. William Crapper set up there instead, nominally as a pork butcher as Stricker's had been. He had hams and black puddings and sausages in his window but, from his window display, he was well stocked with lamb as well.

Maypole. Branson Bowles for Hornby trains. Miss Steele's for Palm Toffee.'

Steve Palmer writes: 'My grandparents' shop in Boothferry Road was Sheppard's Music Shop. The shop was owned by my great-grandfather and then his son, my grandfather Bert, who married the Saturday girl, Alice. She ran the shop while he did repairs to the pianos and radios that were sold there. Bert died in 1958 but Alice lived for many years in Scarborough and only died in 1999 aged 92.'

The post office at number 82 was also Shipley's stationer's and, going back before 1900, the original Mr Shipley had been something of a martinet. A maidservant called Mrs Gelder worked for the Claybourns, butchers, who had a shop at number 88 which later became Fleming's furniture. Mrs Gelder tried to save a little of her wages, although that would have been a struggle. She'd be on

Palm Toffee, made by the London firm of Walters, long gone, came in various guises but the one most people remember is the banana sandwich, a layer of banana-flavoured toffee in between two of standard butter toffee. The bar was thoughtfully divided into squares for easy sharing, which gave everyone the opportunity of having their fillings pulled out.

no more than £20 a year and probably less, at a time when an agricultural labourer was hoping to keep his family on £40 a year.

Anyway, on those pay-days when she felt flush, Mrs Gelder would call in at the post office to deposit a few pennies in her savings account, and Mr Shipley would say 'That's the way to go on'. Alas, if extraordinary circumstances arose that demanded unforeseen expenditure and she had to draw out, Mr Shipley would not approve. He would inform Mrs Gelder that 'This is the road to nowhere'.

Next door, the road led to a branch of another of Goole's butchery families, Willie Crapper's, and then the North Eastern Hotel. Southcott's tailor's was followed by the office of Mr Biller, His Majesty's Inspector of Taxes, the Silver Library, then Holder Brothers' pianos, and a small branch of the Hull Savings Bank – and thereby hangs a tale.

Savings banks were a philanthropic initiative in the late eighteenth and early nineteenth centuries, the idea being to encourage thrift and prudence among the working classes who, naturally, would have no truck with conventional banks. Only the wealthy had bank accounts; the ordinary tradespeople, craftsmen, factory workers and labourers dealt in cash and very little of that. Most such families had nothing to spare but, even so, the savings bank movement gathered pace, based on principles that seem impossible to believe today. Not only would there be no shareholders; nobody working at the bank, which is to say the bankers, would profit from the business.

The Hull bank did well, opened branches around the East Riding and, in 1887, became part of the Trustee Savings Bank Association. These banks didn't really compete with each other – they served their own parts of the country – nor with the orthodox banks, as they were only for cash savings and didn't issue cheque books or allow overdrafts. Much later, in the 1970s, the TSB became a clearing bank like the rest and was taken over by Lloyds in 1995.

Next door to the House of Prudence was the House of Ruin, John Watson's Railway Tavern, then there was Burton, The Tailor of Taste (see page 106), Boots (see page 53 for history of the cash chemist), and the chain butcher, Dewhurst.

At its peak in 1977, Dewhurst had 1,000 shops and more. By 2006, supermarkets had topped 80 per cent of the UK retail meat

William Vestey, 1st Baron Vestey, 1859–1940, was the eldest son of a Yorkshire provision merchant who operated in Liverpool as an importer of American foodstuffs. At the age of 17, William was sent to the USA to find more goods for his father. He set up a factory in Chicago making tins of corned beef, then started sending frozen partridges from Argentina and eggs from China. These little ventures turned into a mammoth business, including the Blue Star shipping line and Dewhurst's butcher's shops.

market and Dewhurst, sold to new owners, was down to less than 100 shops. They went bust in that year. Some of their shops were bought by locals and some, indeed, continued to trade under the Dewhurst name.

The origins of the firm are in the late nineteenth century with two butcher brothers from Liverpool, called Vestey. They were pioneers in several ways, especially in cold storage and importing meat from South America, where they built a vast empire of cattle ranches. At one point they owned Oxo (now Premier Foods), and at another employed 30,000 people, and at another were the richest family in Britain, except they weren't really in Britain because if they had been, they would have had to pay a huge amount of tax. They were an early example of non-doms. There's still a lot of money in the family, although they are said to be down to their last £600 million, and they're friends of royalty, and the Baron Vestey is 22nd in the Order of Precedence of Gentlemen, and they're still in business in a smallish but expanding way, and they grow meat and sugar cane (well, they don't, but somebody does on their behalf), and they have a shipping line, but no butcher's shops.

Next along Goole high street was another chain, Maypole Dairy. George Watson, one of three brothers, opened the first Maypole Dairy shop in Wolverhampton in 1887. It was the dairy that sold no fresh milk and specialised in margarine, but did sell butter. They also had cheese early on, but dropped that to concentrate on margarine, butter, eggs, tea and condensed milk. In 1926, there were 1,000 Maypole Dairies, none of them selling fresh milk, and they were under new management. Grievously wounded in the margarine wars of the early 1920s, the Watsons sold out to Home & Colonial in 1924.

Boots, Dewhurst, Maypole – national names all – then on Boothferry Road came Curry's bicycle shop. Henry Curry, born 1850, set up a bicycle business in Leicester in 1884, the year in which Thomas Stevens set off from San Francisco to ride around the world on a penny-farthing bicycle, a journey that took two years. Meanwhile, Henry was busy building more penny-farthings, also called ordinaries, and a chap called J K Starley, in Coventry, brought out a cycle with almost equally-sized wheels, driven by pedals fixed to a chain. He called it the Rover and it was the first commercially successful safety bicycle. It had solid rubber tyres but that would soon change with an invention by a Scottish vet called Dunlop. Later, the Rover Company made motorbikes, and then cars, which it did until quite recently, but Henry Curry carried on with his bicycles.

It's 1960 and bicycles are on the way out, although most people, including Curry's, don't realise how much of a minority interest they will soon become. Still, television's clearly on the up.

He retired in 1909, passing the business, now with several branches, to his four sons who expanded into electrical goods in the 1920s including the new wireless telegraph receiving sets, or radios. Although television was on the go in 1937, the Goole shop wouldn't have sold any because you couldn't get a signal outside London, but the shop did have toys and gramophones, and bicycles, not made any longer by Curry's themselves but by Hercules with a Curry's badge on.

Television would come later and, with the boosts of the coronation in 1953, the arrival of ITV in 1954 and of colour TV in 1967, Curry's boomed. There were 550 branches in 1984, the year that Dixon's bought the company, keeping the Curry name, which was deemed such a strong one that all the Dixon's shops were later changed to Curry's, or Currys as they have dropped the apostrophe. Now, with PC World in the family, Henry Curry's bicycle legacy is a huge Euro-firm selling squillions of quids' worth

41

of all the latest gear, while Rover bicycles, well, that's another story entirely.

At numbers 44 and 42 Boothferry Road was Marks & Spencer's Bazaar. Having only a vague idea of what a bazaar is supposed to be in this context, your correspondent examined his copy of the *Shorter Oxford English Dictionary*, to find that the word is Persian for market, and by it we mean an oriental marketplace, or a fancy fair for the sale of useful and ornamental articles, usually on behalf of a charitable object. Ah, yes, but this was not just a Women's Institute bazaar. This was an M&S bazaar. See page 104 for M&S history.

Mrs Maisie Raywood, then Miss Greenfield, worked there in the 1920s. She recalled that the hours were long, as they were in every shop, opening early and closing late – nine o'clock on Saturday evenings – and the term 'bazaar' seems to have been well earned. Besides the expected M&S clothing, there were biscuits sold loose from those big square tins, and all sorts of small hardware, the type of thing you get these days in little plastic packets.

Home & Colonial next (see page 69) and the Royal London Mutual Insurance Society, now a massive outfit including Scottish Provident and the Refuge, which in 1937 had its own branch at number 121. There was a cobbler's at number 36, The Cash Boot Co., then Taylor's Drug Co. which had become Timothy White's and Taylor's in 1935 but the sign in Goole hadn't caught up yet.

Lipton's was followed by Freeman, Hardy & Willis, a name that used to be on almost every high street in England. The original shoe shop opened in 1875, somehow hit the right note so a factory was built in Kettering, and in 1929 the firm became part of Sears, which was founded in 1891 by the boot-making brothers Sears using the trade name of Tru-form. Later, they would all be shaken up in a sack by Sir Charles Clore (*qv*), along with Saxone, Dolcis, Lilley & Skinner and others, when these famous names had 3,000 branches between them. FHW (For Happy Walking), subsumed into the British Shoe Corporation and sold on, was partly fragmented into Hush Puppy, turned into Barratt's, and disappeared in 1996. Now, although the market for shoes continues to grow, if only by a little, the sight of a chain shoe shop on the high street is increasingly rare and getting rarer.

Two locals next on Goole high street: Hackforth's grocers with its cafe upstairs, and Blackburn's clothiers. Hackforth's was quite a

No need for pedestrianisation around 1920, apparently. Most of the shops on this stretch of Boothferry Road were still there in 1937 – Meadow Dairy, Blackburn's clothiers, Hackforth's grocer's, Freeman, Hardy & Willis, Lipton's, Taylor's Drugs and the Cash Boot Co. all line up as per, but Mr Spencer the barber, offering electric hair-brushing and ladies' hairdressing by appointment, would be replaced by Hepworth's tailor's. To the left of that at number 18, Jones Sales and their window full of remarkable underwear would be replaced by Maynard's less demanding display of wine gums.

business, with a bakery, grocery and confectionery counters and the cafe staffed by waitresses in green satin uniforms. Tea and a toasted teacake would have cost you sevenpence in the 1920s, which translates as about 3p decimal or about £1 in modern real terms. A roast dinner – the fabled meat and two veg – was a shilling and sixpence, or something over three quid today. Poached egg on toast was the same price as tea and a teacake. If you wanted to go the whole hog, your maximum meal was pork chop, chips and two veg at two shillings and threepence (about a fiver).

Three more chains followed. Meadow Dairy was begun in 1900 and grew to 200 branches by the outbreak of the First World War, like Maypole concentrating on own-label basics – margarine, eggs, butter, lard, tea and tinned milk. 'Meadow Margarine, it tastes like butter, try some today, tenpence a pound.' Home & Colonial bought the firm, and it was to this arm of the H&C empire that Sir Thomas sold Lipton's.

43

Hepworth's tailors (see page 78) was next-door to yet another famous name, Maynard's. Charles Maynard and his brother Tom made sweets by hand for Sarah Maynard, his wife, to sell in the shop. Charles had been doing it since 1880; Charles Junior introduced the wine gum in 1909. Wine gums, of course, contain no wine and never have. Eating them is supposed to be similar to tasting wine, rolling it about the mouth but not spitting it out. Maynard's shops were a familiar and welcome sight on so many high streets, but were taken over by Cadbury's in 1986 and so by Kraft in early 2010. Howsomever, the Maynard's workforce had nothing to fear from Kraft. They did not exist by then, apart from a shop in Filey that has kept the name going but is not of the original strand. Of that, Maynard is nothing more than seven letters on a packet of wine gums.

Coming up to the George IV Inn, after Maynard's and Reno Valet Service on Reno Corner, there was a string of local shops, including Mr Fred Gleadow the hosier and Miss Sarah Gleadow, draper, who was proud to advertise her 'trustworthy underwear', also a tobacconist, another barber, finishing with Frank Crapper, butcher. There we are. That's one side of the street, and not one charity shop, tattoo parlour, building society branch or Chinese take-away, and hardly any provision for ladies' hairdressing, much less unisex hairdressers called Curl Up and Dye. How on earth did they manage in those days?

Across the street, in the run-up to the Cinema Palace, was a series of local shops – grocer, barber, draper, and two sweet shops doing good business even with Maynard's over the road. The National Provincial Bank, the one conventional clearing bank on the whole main street, was a venerable and widespread institution, founded in 1833 with a policy of only having branches outside London. Within 65 miles of the capital, 'The Old Lady of Threadneedle Street' had the monopoly of issuing banknotes. So long as the National Provincial kept beyond that circle, it could issue banknotes too. The first branch was in Gloucester but by a strategy of acquiring small, local banks and opening up in virgin territory, the bank had about 250 branches by the time Queen Victoria died.

After the First World War, a merger with the Union of London and Smith's Bank almost doubled the number of branches but we do not know how many, like the Goole one, had a doctor's surgery inside. After the Second World War there were various takeovers and sellings-off but a merger with the District Bank in 1962 and the Westminster Bank in 1968 produced a company with thousands of branches and a new name, the National Westminster. In 2000 it was taken over by the much smaller Royal Bank of Scotland and the rest doesn't bear thinking about.

Next door to the bank on Boothferry Road was Huggins's iron-monger, then Rockett's draper for confident customers. If you wanted the lady manager, the owner's sister, to fetch you some-thing out of the window display, you had to be self-assured or very thick-skinned if you then decided not to buy it. Curran's electrical was down the side and upstairs, then came the fearless voice of *The Goole Times*. Journalists could buy their cakes and pies at Newel and Tasker, bakers, later the electricity board showrooms, and their woollen swimming costumes from Philip Seltzer, Athletic Outfitter.

Here are David Lea-Jackson's memories: 'Goole had gas lighting and you would see the lighter guy riding around town with a long pole over his shoulder. I remember Hackforth's, although I could never remember what was on the ground floor. Branson Bowles had ladies' fashions with the added attraction, for small boys that is, of Dinky toys around the window base. There was a little shop that stocked Tootal ties and cravats of which I had a considerable number. Another shop was Seltzer's, just before Woolworth's. I'm not sure what they sold but have a feeling it was leather goods, not for the faint-hearted.'

Geoff LeVoguer: 'I remember Mr Seltzer well. I believe he was of Jewish extraction. His meticulously well stocked shop sold the latest swimming trunks, sports kits, air guns, leather goods and all manner of knives. I bought my first pair of continental football boots there. His shop sold Real Madrid football kits when Ferenc Puskas's magical side were the kings of Europe.'

Martin Schultz: 'My grandfather, Philip Seltzer, was the owner of Seltzer's Leather Store. I recall visiting the shop when I was a child. It was a shame that the shop was forced to close in the 1970s when the lease expired. He went to run the Sports Goods Department in Northern Clothing until he retired.'

Miriam Schultz: 'My grandparents owned and ran Seltzer's. Every Saturday we went from Hull by car with our mum to collect my grandparents. It was the weekly treat. The shop was an Aladdin's cave. On the right-hand side were stepped shelves from waist height almost to the ceiling, stacked with toys of all shapes, sizes and prices. The end wall had the same stepped shelves but with horse brasses and household ornaments, and the left-hand wall was filled from floor to ceiling with sports goods, such as fishing rods and tackle, tennis racquets and every sort of ball. My granddad also would re-string tennis racquets in the back of the shop with catgut which, of course, I thought was really cats' guts. They also stocked guns, I think, and shot.'

Ms Schultz needed only to adjust her thoughts slightly. Her granddad was certainly using gut to re-string racquets, and it was and still is called catgut, but it's not from cats. It's almost always from sheep, and is intestines cured in ancient ways to be used in musical instruments as well as racquets. The best violin strings are made in Italy, called Roman strings, and the toughest guts come from the hardiest, scrawniest sheep. The cat confusion may come from 'kit', the name of an old-fashioned style of small fiddle used in dancing classes, or it may not.

While Mr Seltzer was singing his merry racquet-stringing song, Hepworth's (no relation) next door was selling tobacco. Mr Boom was outfitting gentlemen at number 31, and above him was the Unemployment Assistance Board. This was a relatively new body, created by a 1934 Act, which was a national agency to relieve poverty among those unemployed who had not been part of the National Insurance scheme. Unemployment was around 10 per cent at the time, although the types of job you might or might not get were very different from today. Much, much greater numbers worked on the land and in mundane factory jobs, and in domestic service. Those who had not paid National Insurance contributions could call at number 31 Boothferry Road, above Boom's, and be subjected to the hated Household Means Test. The government of the day wanted to alleviate poverty, but it didn't want to encourage idleness or give succour to the workshy. The latter concern may have outweighed the former in some cases, and being awarded much dole over and above money to pay the rent was not common.

Another new name, put up in 1933, was the F W Woolworth Bazaar (see page 148) at numbers 35 and 37, more properly known as the Woolworth 3d and 6d Store, or Woolies. The American idea of five cents and ten cents pricing was here translated into three-pence and sixpence. For more expensive items such as a camera costing one and six (7½p, or about £4 in real terms) the rule of 'Nothing over 6d' was circumnavigated by selling the thing in three pieces costing 6d each. The other great innovation was having the goods on open display where customers could examine them, rather than having to ask an assistant.

Tracy Partington writes: 'I remember a lot of those shops, Lipton's, Freeman Hardy & Willis, Boots, *Goole Times*, Yorkshire Electricity Board, Marks & Spencer's. What's now Wetherspoon's was a bank and there was a market on the outside bit at the back of Woolworth's. There was Altham's at the other end of Boothferry Road and the cinema with the sweet shop next door with all kinds of sweets.'

Six local shops followed Woolworth's – cleaner (Holroyd, later Zerny's), ladies' outfitter, cycle shop, dress shop, jeweller, watch-maker, the small chain Kettering and Leicester Boot Co., local draper Sargentson, the Station Hotel and one of the biggest local shops, the draper Branson Bowles which, as noted elsewhere, had the idea of selling toys for boys, presumably to keep them quiet while Modom was choosing her gown.

There was a tobacconist, Mr Nickless, at number 75 followed by Johnson's, dyers and cleaners. This firm was quite a large chain, begun as silk dyers in Liverpool in 1817 but going into dry-cleaning in a determined way in the 1920s. Today, Johnson's claim to be the biggest in the business with over 500 shops, one of which is at 39–41 Boothferry Road, where the Home & Colonial used to be.

In 1937, another sweet shop, another grocer's and a wallpaper shop came, we think, before The Public Benefit Boot and Shoe Company, which had a branch in Goole but there is conflicting information about where it was. It may have been 33 or 83 Booth-ferry Road at some time, but in any case it was part of a chain of 200 or more that began with a small shop in Hull in 1875, owned by William Franklin. Their trademark was a picture of a giant boot on a horse-drawn cart, a relic of the days when a real giant boot was trotted around Yorkshire as an advertising gimmick.

Next door to the cheap boots was a pawnbroker, George Kelshaw, then another sweet shop, an architect's office above a boot and shoe

The children pictured are not, as you might have imagined, auditioning for parts in *The Midwich Cuckoos* but doing their bit for the Leeds Infirmary by taking part in a doll-dressing. Beneath the notice proclaiming the dress-in by twelve Goole schoolgirls, the only boy does not have a doll and stares at the camera with calm indifference to that fact and to his being surrounded by females. Perhaps he is expecting to be allowed a go with one of the magic lanterns, or the clockwork Hornby engine. Branson Bowles was founded in 1895; in 1946 twenty people worked there in what amounted to a small department store, later a branch of Wetherell's of Selby (which is still there, in Selby anyway).

shop, then Jackson's Stores, house furnishers, Airey's butchers, the (Cosy) Carlton Cinema and the Modern Library.

Before the Public Libraries Act of 1919, municipal libraries were much restricted by a penny rate cap, which meant only the large cities could collect enough money to buy quantities of books and pay librarians. In the smaller towns, W H Smith, Boots and others were the library providers, and in rural areas, that is about half the country, there was no library service at all. Great progress was made after the Act put public libraries into the hands of the counties and set going an all-embracing system of co-operation and free borrowing which eventually meant the end of the private circulating libraries.

People of the post-war generations may have often wondered why so many of their parents and elders, especially those not of the upper classes, were apt to furnish themselves with false teeth when still relatively young. The answer lies with fellows like Mr George Hall, dentist, at number 119, between Eastham's furniture shop and the Refuge Assurance Co. Mr Hall, though doubtless well-meaning and highly skilled, was deeply handicapped by the equipment of the age. The electric drill had yet to reach affordable perfection – this was before the NHS, remember – and so was largely unknown except in the more expensive practices and America. First patented in the 1870s, the early electric and clockwork drills, which super-seded the simple drill bit twirled between finger and thumb, were themselves quickly outclassed by the foot-treadle drill, which whirled at 2000 rpm. This is probably the one Mr Hall would have used, powered by himself, with the inevitable variations in drill direction and pressure accompanying his forward leanings into the treadle.

This is why so many people preferred extraction under general anaesthetic, which dentists could administer then, to fillings with a novocaine injection which itself was an unpleasant experience. And now they're talking about doing away with drills and fillings altogether, and healing by painless plasma jet (whatever that is). They don't know they're born these days.

Well, we're nearly at the end of the business premises, and here's a surprise. Number 123, Walter Martin, ladies' hairdresser, and another, T Cook and Son, physiotherapists. Last at number 169 was Dr Cretney, later to move into the National Provincial Bank.

That was Goole high street in 1937. In other streets there were shops for fish, tools, tripe, poultry food and so on. There were more ladies' hairdressers and grocers. There was an aerated waters manufacturer and a wireless dealer. It could have been anywhere in Britain, but everywhere in Britain it would have been different. Yes, there would have been a Woolies and a W H Smith and a Boots, but you could have looked at it and remembered it as Goole, or Middlesbrough, or Sidmouth, or Norwich, or wherever.

Your correspondent recalls walking down the high street at Berwick-upon-Tweed. It would have been around 1972. In the memory are ten butcher's shops, or at least six at any rate, all with fantastic displays of pies and white puddings and black puddings and many kinds of mysterious Northumberland and Scottish sausages. Any southerner (that is, anyone from south of the A66)

Boothferry Road, Goole, twenty-first century. As Miss Joni Mitchell sang in 1970, *Don't it always seem to go, that you don't know what you've got till it's gone. They paved paradise, and put up a parking lot.*

could have spent hours gazing in these windows, trying to work out what everything was. Not now, my friends, not now. Now, you would hardly know the difference between Cardiff and Nottingham.

CHAPTER 3

Great shopsters of the high streets

James Aitchison

It seems that the first use of a piece of glass to help with reading the small print occurred before there was any print (in Europe, anyway). Roger Bacon, the Franciscan monk, imprisoned for his ungodly attempts to explain natural phenomena by means of science and for having the temerity to invent things, wrote of the magnifying qualities of glass in 1266. Presumably the usefulness of his discovery came to outweigh religious scruples because, in 1352, an Italian cardinal was depicted in a Treviso church fresco with a pair of specs.

Progress in this connection was slow, because there was hardly any need for it. Only monks and other churchmen and a few of the nobility learned to read, they being the only ones who ever saw a book until printing came along. By 1600, literacy and books were much more usual, and selling glasses became a viable trade for a high street shop. Charles I granted a charter to the Spectacle Makers' Guild in 1629, and efforts were concentrated on difficult matters such as making a really good lens through which you could see properly.

Still, the term 'optician' was not used in this sense. An optician was one who was knowledgeable in the optical division of natural science. In 1737, the term was first used to mean a maker of optical instruments, but mainly implying telescopes and suchlike. Around that time, the son and grandson of a French immigrant silk weaver were taking an interest in this branch of physics. John Dollond and his boy Peter both worked at the weaver's trade but gave that up in favour of Dollond & Son, in the Strand, London, at the sign of the Golden Spectacles and Sea Quadrant.

John Dollond's speciality was telescopes, particularly making them much smaller and more effective. He had papers read to The Royal Society and in 1761 was elected a Fellow, having already been given a medal. He died later the same year and son Peter took on the business in a much more commercial way, steering it through several patent disputes in the courts. He joined up with his younger brother, also John, and moved shop to St Paul's Churchyard. There they made instruments for Captain Cook and the first telescopes cased in mahogany instead of vellum. Later they introduced the now familiar sliding, contracting brass types which do, in fact, telescope.

Strictly speaking, the direct family connection ended with the deaths of the two brothers but a nephew, George Huggins, had become a partner and in recognition of the excellent reputation of P and J Dollond, changed his name accordingly. He was an inventor too, much improving micrometers and ships' compasses, became FRS and optician to Queen Victoria, and was awarded a medal for devising a weather station that recorded temperature, rain, wind and so on automatically, on a roll of paper.

George Dollond had not worked at the weaver's trade but he was a bachelor and lived by himself, so when he died the business went to another nephew, also a Huggins, who also changed his name to Dollond. His son sold the firm in 1871 to one of the workers there, a Mr Chant, who didn't change his own name but kept the company's when he moved to Ludgate Hill.

He would have noted carefully the new optician's shop opening in Fleet Street, not far away, in 1889, and perhaps have been taken aback by this young man James Aitchison, hardly out of his apprenticeship, selling pairs of glasses at a shilling, and half a crown for the personally fitted ones. As if that were not enough, the upstart also committed the venial sin of advertising, considered deeply unprofessional, and thereby soon had three branches in London and one in Leeds. He offered 'Spectacles, Eyeglasses and Artificial Eyes at most moderate prices'. Mr Aitchison's system of Sight-Testing was stated to be the most perfect in existence. His patent folding pocket binocular field glasses were similarly the most useful in existence, and could be carried in the waistcoat pocket.

He died suddenly, aged only 51, in 1911. His son Irvine changed the family firm to a limited company in 1912 and introduced the owl trademark and the slogan 'Are your eyes right?'.

Both companies, Dollond's and Aitchison's, struggled after the First World War and in 1927 Irvine Aitchison bought Dolland and Co. The great leap forward came after the next war, when Clement Attlee's Labour government introduced free eye tests and glasses under the National Health Service. Never had there been such a demand and the opticians coined it, despite the ghastly frames of the free glasses. How your correspondent hated his round wire specs with the curly ends that made his ears sore, and how amazed he stood when John Lennon made them fashionable.

Dollond and Aitchison became a public company in 1953, then went through several ownership phases until finally merging with Boots Opticians in 2009, to create a network of almost 700 shops. It is envisaged, says the official blurb, that the Dollond and Aitchison name will disappear beneath Boots, so, goodbye owl.

Jesse Boot

Nobody did more than Jesse Boot, and very, very few have done nearly as much, to define the character and set down the pattern of our high streets. Like other great shop-founders such as Burton, Smith, Lipton and Marks, Boot began with almost nothing and, particularly like Burton and Lipton, one big idea: that to sell vast quantities of goods at reasonable prices to the great British public was a far more exciting and enriching prospect than bowing and scraping before the carriage trade.

Willoughby-on-the-Wolds, rural Nottinghamshire, 1849: a farm labourer and lay preacher, John Boot, was forced by ill health to give up his work. John was a self-educated man, well versed in the medicinal qualities of herbs. As well as his ministry work, he had, in effect, filled the bill as village doctor and chemist to those who could not afford the professionally qualified real thing, which was everybody except the gentry. Now unable to do heavy manual jobs, it seemed logical to use his herbalist's skills where there were more patients, so he and his wife moved the 10 miles or so to the big

city, Nottingham, to Goose Gate, where they opened a small shop, grandiosely titled The British and American Botanic Establishment. A few months later, Jesse was born.

As young Jesse grew up, he used to go with his father on herb-gathering expeditions and a planned succession seemed laid out for the boy, but father died in 1860 with Jesse just 10 years old and sister Jane only a toddler of 2. Widow Mary ran the shop, with Jesse taking on increasing responsibility but finding that his mother was not open to his adventurous and expansive ideas. In those times, the sense of ordained place in society was very great. It took enormous bravura, revolutionary fervour and ambition, what Burton and Marks might have called double extra *chutzpah*, to break out and away. Mary Boot didn't have that, but Jesse did. Even so, as long as the firm was M & J Boot, it stayed where it was and Jesse had to keep his ambitions reined in.

By 1877 he was in sole charge and began taking on the Nottingham chemist establishment, buying in bulk and selling for cash to the poorer mass of the people, and taking large advertising spaces in the local press. On one famous occasion, he bought a ton of Epsom salts and dragooned the family and anybody else he could find into packing it into 2,240 pound bags, sufficient, as it turned out, for only two weeks. The shop window was filled with it, from top to bottom. The normal price in Nottingham was a halfpenny an ounce. Jesse offered it at a penny a pound, an eighth (12.5%) of the going rate, and 500 bags for a Saturday's trade were hardly enough.

Epsom salts, by the way and for younger readers, chemical name magnesium sulphate heptahydrate, was a highly regarded cure-all in those days. Most people took it orally; it works as a laxative and, like many such, was therefore thought to be of general benefit to health. In modern times, it features largely as bath salts with several different benefits claimed. At Jesse's prices, the citizens of Nottingham could take a glass of it each morning and put handfuls of the stuff in the tin bath on a Friday night.

Also for the weekly bath, soft soap usually cost fourpence a pound. Boot had it at fourpence ha'penny for two pounds. We have to remember that such sensational bargains were not at all the accepted thing among traders. We are used to buy one, get one free, and half price on this and that, and loss leaders. The good folk of Nottingham in 1880 had never seen anything like it, and nor had the other shop-keepers, the other chemists, and the burghers on the town council. They, the traditional trading classes, believed it couldn't last, that the parvenu Boot would very soon crash, and they spread stories that his bargains were impossible without adulterated goods and shady dealings.

Well, Jesse was a dealer all right, and not just in salts and soap. He had a chance to buy a frighteningly large quantity of tins of salmon, and he didn't frighten easily. There were thirty-six tins in a case, usual price eightpence a tin. On the first Saturday they sold forty cases at not quite half price, fourpence ha'penny. As a great many working-class homes didn't have a tin opener, Jesse had to employ a man to do nothing else but open tins of salmon, from eight in the morning to half past ten at night. These were Saturday hours. Other days they closed early, at eight o'clock.

Success demanded more space, so Jesse rebuilt the shop in 1882. Soon afterwards his mother died, the firm became Boot and Co. Ltd., and moved into other parts of Nottingham. In 1884 he opened up in Sheffield and Lincoln. In 1885, the first factory started work, in Island Street, Nottingham, and then came the shock. In 1886, exhausted by working eighteen hours a day minimum, his only time off being his several visits to the Methodist chapel on a Sunday, Jesse Boot was on the verge of a breakdown. He knew it, too. At the age of 36, he decided to sell up.

John Boot's shop, opened in 1849 in Goose Gate, Nottingham. It became Jesse's own, and the platform for his near incredible journey, in 1877, which is when this photograph was taken.

PATENT MEDICINES

AND

HOUSEHOLD ARTICLES.

Adams' Furniture Polish, 8d. size for 6d , 1/2 for 10d.

Allen's Hair Restorer. 6/- for 3/4½

Allcock's Plasters. 13½d size for 7d.

Bond's Marking Ink, 6d. for 3d., 1/- for 6d.

Borax lump, 7d. per lb., ground 8d.

Coal Tar Soap, five 6d. tablets for 1/-

Cream of Tartar, 4d. quarter lb , 1 3 per lb.

Camphorated Chalk, 4½d. per quarter lb.

Epsom Salts, 2d. per lb., 7 lbs. for 1 -

Eno's Fruit Salt, 2/9 bottle for 2/-

Freidrichshall Bitter Water, 1 4 bottle for 11d.

Hunyadi Janos Water, 2/- size for 1 3, 14/6 per doz.

Jewsbury's Oriental Tooth Paste, 1/6 for 10d½., 2/6
    for 1/4

Lamplough's Pyretic Saline. 2 6 size for 1/9.

Mother Siegel's Syrup, 2/6 bottles for 1/10

Quinine Wine, 2/6 size for 2/-

Rooke's Oriental Pills, 13½d. size for 8½d.

Whelpton's Pills, 13½d. size for 8½d.

Woodward's Gripe Water, 13½d. size for 9d.

Woodward's Gripe Water, 2/8 size (great saving)
    for 1/10

All other Patent Medicines at equally cheap rates.

Coal tar soap, five for the price of two, ink half price, hair restorer and plasters
very nearly half price, Mother Siegel's Syrup, eightpence off – this was Jesse Boot
and his outrageous sales tactics in about 1880.

Sister Jane persuaded him to take a holiday instead, to Jersey, and there he met a bookseller's daughter, Florence Rowe. They married and, with twice the business brains and twice the energy, Mr and Mrs Boot and the renamed Boots Pure Drug Company set out on their amazing adventure, from ten shops in 1890 to 550 in 1914, and the fulfilment of a brilliant notion: chemist as department store. Florence ran the Number Two department – toiletries, fancy goods, art, stationery. There were books also, mostly devotional at first, later to develop into the twopenny Booklovers' Libraries. She travelled over Europe looking for new lines at sensible prices, and the Boots opened shops far larger than any chemist ever thought of, with lifts and electric light.

Manufacturing kept pace too, and research chemists were brought in. Florence was especially keen on staff welfare. Many of their factory workers were women from poor households. When she heard that it was usual to come to work without breakfast, she introduced free hot cocoa to start the day. Like Burton, the Boots understood the importance of a happy and healthy workforce, introducing staff outings, sports, and all manner of welfare facilities that we take for granted today but were novelties then.

All this had been achieved against considerable opposition, from the pharmaceutical establishment and from similarly entre-preneurial chains of chemist's shops, such as Taylor's Drug Stores of Leeds, Timothy White's in the south-west, and Day's in London, although they didn't go quite so boldly for size and glamour in their premises. Jesse Boot's response to their competition was typical. He forged partnerships with like-minded men; for example conquering Lancashire with a grocer, James Duckworth. Otherwise, if he couldn't beat them, he bought them, acquiring Campbell's of Norwich in 1894, and Day's sixty-five shops in 1901. Timothy White's and Taylor's would have to wait until 1968.

We are inclined to think of the commercialisation of Christmas as a fairly recent thing. If we do think so, we are quite wrong. The deeply Christian and rather puritanical Jesse Boot, in 1904, took the whole front page of the *Daily Mail* for ten consecutive days to advertise his Christmas wares, and eight full pages of *The Times*, and more in the main provincial dailies. So good were the results that the Boots Christmas campaign became a national institution, and Jesse could state in his 1907 Christmas ads that 'We have

Timothy White's, 'The English firm', is opposite Boots (the Nottingham firm), and Maynard Toffee Maker faces MacFisheries in Woking, sometime in the 1930s. Punch cigars were an authentic Cuban make, popular with those who liked their cigars to be noticeable.

branches in all the principal towns, and are the largest gift sellers in the country'.

Many of the gifts were toiletries, packed in expensive (well, expensive-looking) bottles and jars. One of the ploys was to invent a proprietary name, put a signature on the label, and take such liberties with trade descriptions, common practice at the time, as would have your modern standards inspectors fainting in disbelief. For instance, there was a fictional benefactor of mankind called Girard, who developed a secret formula for a wonder face cream. 'Girard's Glycerin, Cucumber and Honey Cream, exclusive to Boots, none genuine without the signature', contained no cucumber or honey but it came in a nice pot. Boots own Egg Julep, a kind of shampoo, was just a solution of soap and potassium carbonate, which would make the soap froth up more by softening the water, and yellow dye.

In 1909, the farm labourer's boy was made Sir Jesse. In recognition of war service to the nation, manufacturing great amounts of medicines for the troops, in 1917 he was made a baronet. All was not well, however. He suffered terribly from arthritis and was looking to retire. The problem, as he saw it, was that he could not identify a reliable successor to carry the business onwards and upwards. Jesse also suffered from wood-and-trees syndrome and, quite unable to discern the right qualities in his son John, sold the lot to the American United Drug Company in 1920.

Jesse Boot had to wait a long time to get really moving. The advertisement (see opposite) is from 1893, when Jesse was 43 or 44, and there was no stopping him thereafter. The farm labourer's son, progenitor of a thousand shops, became Sir Jesse in 1909 and later my Lord of Trent, and he sold out to Americans in 1920 because he didn't believe his own son was up to the mark.

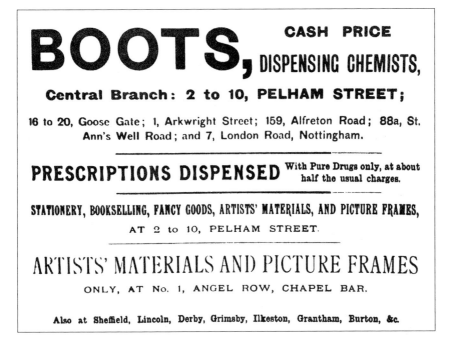

Under their dynamic management, Boots prospered and, much to father's disbelief, made son John chairman in 1926. In 1929, Jesse became the first Lord Trent and died in 1931, aged 81. Two years later, son John launched a management buyout and retook Boots for Britain. The 1,000th branch was opened in the same year, in Galashiels, by Florence, Lady Trent.

Nowadays, Boots is merged with Alliance Unichem with branches all over the world, 140 in Thailand, for instance, and one in the new mall in Dubai. And what, we have to wonder, would Mrs Mary Boot have thought of that?

Clemens and August Brenninkmeijer

The German family of Brenninkmeijer were farmers who, from the 1600s, also traded in linen and wool in Mettingen, 40 miles or so from the Dutch border. By 1840, two Brenninkmeijer brothers had established themselves as travellers in textiles and they decided they needed a solid trading base. They chose Sneek, a modest town in the Friesland province of Holland, and opened a warehouse there in 1841, calling their company C&A from their first-name initials.

As the business developed they, like quite a few of our high street pioneers, saw an opportunity in ready-made clothes in standard sizes, aimed at the great mass of people who were not wealthy enough to expect their tailors and dressmakers to call at the house.

In 1861 the brothers opened a shop in Sneek, and soon went on to open more in other Dutch towns and cities. From the very beginnings, the philosophy was to look after staff well, with good conditions and pensions and, in return, to expect loyalty and confidentiality, and soundness of morality. They were a Roman Catholic family in a Protestant country and their business was run according to high principles and a strict code of conduct. Another founding precept that would last for the duration was secrecy. Newspapers were for advertising only, not for editorial. C&A would have no spokespersons and no PR department. Theirs was a private company, minding its own business and, even in the modern media era, nobody gives interviews.

The expansion of the firm was managed without the usual corporate trappings of head office and directors of a limited company. It was all in the family, with no outside shareholders. Some members went back into Germany in 1911 and opened a store in Berlin. After the First World War they also opened in Britain, in 1922, in London's Oxford Street, where the store was called C&A Modes.

The plan was one with which we are very familiar today – to offer fashionable clothes, ready made, at reasonable prices – but in those days it was revolutionary. Fashion had been the preserve of the rich and, preferably, idle. Nobody had thought the idea realistic, that a girl who was no more than a clerk in an office, or an assistant in a shop, could afford to follow changing trends and dress like her betters.

Liverpool came next, in 1924, then Birmingham and Manchester. The Second World War set the firm back a bit, but they had negotiated their way out of a ban in Germany on foreign-owned businesses and were strong in the UK, and so they had a platform for expansion from the early 1960s onwards, into Belgium, France, Switzerland, Spain, Austria and, more recently, Poland, Hungary, Russia, Romania, Croatia ... but wait a moment. Here is one of the self-proclaimed leading companies in European retailing and one of the wealthiest business dynasties ever, and they don't now have a store in the UK.

The reason for their withdrawal lay in their founding principles. They liked big, central, high street locations for their massive stores, selling low-cost garments (including menswear from 1957. Remember 'Man at C&A'?). These shops were very expensive to run, and competition was getting fierce in the middle and at the lower end of the market. Marks & Spencer was one very strong competitor, and chains such as Next, Topshop and Miss Selfridge were stealing customers.

The image of C&A was so clearly defined in British minds that the firm had little hope of reinventing itself for the twenty-first century. On mainland Europe, the family may have felt more at home, and certainly their establishment in Holland and Germany seemed much more solid. So C&A announced its intentions in 2000 and within a year had decamped entirely from these shores, closing 120 shops. Now they have over 1,300 stores in Europe, and more than 30,000 staff. The gap left behind in the UK has been filled by companies like Primark.

Charles Clore

Charlie Clore was not a high street hero. He never kept a shop or even worked in one, much less worked every hour God sent like Jesse Boot, but he did have a colourful life and he did end up owning huge chunks of our high streets, so we'll have him in.

Charles was the second youngest of seven children, born in 1904 in the East End to Russian immigrants Israel Clore and Yetta Abrahams, who were in the textile trade. Charlie didn't think much of that so, after elementary school, he didn't stick his dad's business long before going off to South Africa to seek his fortune. He came back after three years not having found it but with his dealer's instincts undimmed.

The sporting sensation that year, 1927, was the heavyweight boxing World Championship fight, a return match between Gene Tunney and Jack Dempsey, the Manassa Mauler who had held the title from 1919 to 1926. In the seventh round, Dempsey knocked Tunney down but was slow to move to a neutral corner. Tunney got up on thirteen and, in the tenth, knocked out Dempsey. A film had been made of the fight and Charlie bought the rights to show it in South Africa. He sold the rights on at a profit, and looked for his next bargain.

It turned out to be a skating rink, followed by a theatre, some factories, a casino and shares in a gold-mining company. He didn't acquire any retail premises until 1946, when he bought the thirty Richard Shops and a department store in Reading, Heelas (now John Lewis). He can't have had much to do with any of his businesses as businesses, seeing them only as something relatively cheap that he could sell on for more, for instance, Furness Ship-builders that he later sold to Swan Hunter.

Our chief interest came about in 1953 when he bought 70 per cent of Sears, a firm with several boot and shoe factories and no less than 900 shops. Until that time, takeovers had usually been gentlemanly matters, with directors of the target company agreeing terms with he who would have their assets. Often, the outfit being taken over was weak in some way and would benefit from a new liaison. But that wasn't Charlie Clore's method. There was nothing especially wrong with Sears, except Clore thought the shares undervalued because the management was not making the most of its opportunities, so he went straight to the share-holders with an offer they couldn't refuse, ignoring the protesting directors completely.

After more deals, he ended up with thousands of shoe shops, a quarter of the whole UK shoe trade, and a few other names too. Look along your high street in, let's say, 1970, and you might have seen Tru-form, Saxone, Dolcis, Lilley & Skinner, Freeman, Hardy & Willis, Mappin & Webb, Lewis's, Selfridge's, and William Hill. They all belonged to Charlie Clore.

He was a driven man, utterly intolerant of weakness in others. Since almost everyone had weaknesses except Charles Clore, this meant he was intolerant full stop. He could not understand why his wife, Francine Halphen, a French resistance heroine, insisted on a divorce, nor could he understand why money did not buy happiness. It did buy him an endless stream of sexual conquests (conquest probably being the right word), triumphs on the race track, a superb art collection and, after far too long a wait in his view, a knighthood. That is, bought in the sense that very rich people are often knighted, especially if they give lots away, as

Charles Clore did. He retired to Monte Carlo and died of cancer in 1979 leaving many charitable bequests including the Clore Gallery at the Tate, to house the Turner collection.

William Debenham

In the year 2000, October thereof, not April 1st, *The Guardian* reported the startling news that, despite the name of Debenham being associated with department stores throughout the land for 150 years, nobody called Debenham had ever been associated with the firm. The originator of it all, Clement Freebody, had felt insecure in having only one name, competing as he was with Swan & Edgar, Marshall & Snelgrove, Harvey (and) Nichols, Lewis & Allenby, *et cetera*, so he added the name of his home village in Suffolk. This story is so gloriously wrong that it ought to have won a prize.

A draper's shop at 44 Wigmore Street started trading in 1778 but the real beginnings of Debenham's were in 1813, when the incumbent, a man called Thomas Clark who sold expensively fashionable apparel to gentlewomen, met William Debenham. This William had several positive aspects to him, from Thomas Clark's point of view. He had connections with and experience in the manufacturing side of the trade. He had similar connections and some experience in the City. And he had £500 cash to invest in a partnership.

Debenham was a Suffolk boy, although from Sudbury way, not Debenham, born in 1794. Coming along so much earlier than Jesse Boot and the other pioneers of working-class shopping, William never saw things their way. He saw only the money to be made from the wealthy, especially the *nouveaux riches* whose lady folk were so anxious to keep up with not so much the Joneses as the gilded *jeunesses* of the nobility.

The new partnership had a stroke of luck when the fashion for formal mourning migrated down from royalty and the upper aristocracy to those in society who were merely well funded. Now, when daddy died, mummy, daughters and granddaughters all had to have several black outfits in the latest styles, and the more expensive these outfits, the sadder the ladies could be seen to have been at their patron's passing.

Soon, Clark and Debenham's shop at No 44 was mirrored by Debenham and Clark's shop opposite, and the house at No 42 became the Debenham residence, William having married Miss Caroline Freebody and begun a sequence of ten children, including William junior in 1824 and Frank in 1837. All went swimmingly for a number of years. Clark retired, Debenham carried on, and another social trend became apparent. Some of the towns outside London, even those in the far north beyond the Arctic Circle such as Chester and Harrogate, had shops that were being supplied with the latest and finest ladies' clothes. Residents of these towns no longer had to send to London. They could buy locally. William decided he had to get in there, and the first out-of-London Debenham's was set up in exactly that sort of town, Cheltenham, with brother-in-law Clement Freebody running it. In 1851 the firm reformed as Debenham & Freebody with Clement and son William in the partnership.

Old father William died in 1863 and Clement a few years after, leaving junior William and younger brother Frank in charge. Frank was the dynamo. While William diverted much of his attention to promoting homeopathic medicine, Frank expanded the business rapidly, importing the best fabrics from the continent and going into manufacturing and wholesaling. He instituted departments for all the different types of fashion line, acquired other retailers and invigorated the export trade to the Empire. His son – William's marriage was childless as well as homeopathic – proved to be a chip off the old block and, after Marlborough and Trinity College, Cambridge, Ernest Ridley Debenham joined the firm at age 27. He married Cecily Kenrick in 1892 and moved to a fine new house in Kensington.

The end of the century was approaching. The store needed a facelift and the business needed to reassess its priorities in the face of ever increasing competition, which was draining away some of the most valued customers. Debenham & Company was born, and a new store was opened in 1906. Frank retired in 1912 and Ernest took over.

The First World War affected retailing in different ways. It was the making of some businesses but certainly not of the luxury fashion department stores. Debenham's struggled, as did all the others, and Ernest decided to reduce the competition for what little trade there was by collaborating and turning a rival into a partner. He selected Marshall & Snelgrove as his ideal, and their engagement in 1916 turned into marriage in 1919. Another new member of the family in 1920 was Harvey Nichols.

Sir Ernest Ridley Debenham, Bart., as he would become in 1931, was an old-style boss, paternalistic but no delegator. He was keen on education for his workers and started several schemes for that purpose, and instituted various health and welfare improvements, but illustrated his slightly feudal outlook by writing to all ex-employees serving in the war, telling them that they could re-apply for their posts at the end of hostilities, subject to a medical.

Apart from business, Ernest's greatest love was his 10,000-acre estate in Dorset, centred on the hamlet of Braintspuddle and the larger village of Affpuddle, which are on the River Puddle, also known as the Piddle, downstream from Puddletown, upstream of Turnerspuddle, and not far from Tolpuddle. His idea was to develop an entirely self-sufficient agricultural enterprise along the most modern lines, innovating scientifically where traditional methods could be improved. He believed that the more a farm produced, the more workers could be employed on it.

The war interrupted his plan but soon afterwards he was busy, having forty or so cottages built in Braintspuddle, each with indoor lavatory and bathroom and a quarter-acre garden, designed according to custom and practice in that region, to make a kind of new-old model village. Estate employees lived in the cottages and everything was hunky-dory, except the estate never made any money even though it was years ahead of its time in farming practice; for instance, setting new standards in milk hygiene. Ernest's Grade A milk was the first to be put into waxed cartons commercially.

Rather, the whole venture required constant topping up from Ernest and he, having sold his interest in the store thus ending all family connections, had only his capital to live on. Admittedly that was the 1927 equivalent of about £200 million but estates can be terribly costly. As milk prices dropped, he had to let a few farms and stop building. Possibly worse, he had to watch employment go down with increased and more efficient production, rather than up as he had thought. He died at Moor Lane House, in his beloved Braintspuddle, in 1952.

Debenham's meanwhile had added more and more provincial stores to the group, many of them continuing to trade under

DEBENHAM & CO

wish to inform readers that shopping
in our new premises is a real pleasure.
The new club room, writing room, cloak rooms
and restaurant are now open.

ROYAL ERMINE BOLERO

with wing sleeves and Vest of purple velvet,
embroidered with silver cord, from £60.

Taking an average between the retail price index and average earnings from 1907
to the present day, that's about £15,000. Better buy artificial.

their own names and in their own ways. There were 110 stores after the Second World War. Some in Scotland were sold to Harrod's, a failed attempt was made on House of Fraser, fifty Cresta stores were bought, unprofitable provincial stores were closed, a takeover bid by United Drapery Stores was repulsed, and the Burton Group bought what was left, sixty-five stores, in 1985. Debenham's was demerged in 1998 as Burton became Arcadia, and was bought by a private consortium in 2003. There are now about 200 stores altogether, forty of them franchises abroad including stores in Iran, Vietnam and all sorts of other unlikely places. And all because a young fellow from Suffolk invested £500 in a small draper's shop.

Julius Charles Drew

... had a kind of parallel business life with Thomas Lipton (*qv*), and the parallel lines were eventually to join. Julius Drew was from Pulloxhill, near Ampthill, Bedfordshire, born 1856, one of eight (or possibly seven) children of a clergyman, the Reverend George Drew, and Mary, née Peek, whose family was in tea. Julius went into the tea business through his uncle's firm, Peek and Winch, which sent him from his boarding school in Bournemouth to China, as a tea buyer.

He came back in 1877, worked in the offices in Liverpool for a while, then opened his own Willow Pattern Tea Store there, and another in London in 1883 under an inspired new name, The Home & Colonial Stores. Drew the tea expert now had a business partner, John Musker, a retailing wizard and, in a very few years, they had built such a chain of shops that they could go public in 1888 and retire as rich men and significant shareholders in the company they had founded.

Julius Drew had a mission, and it wasn't to do with tea. He was convinced that he was the scion of the family of Drogo, or Dru, that had come over with the Conqueror but had somehow lost its Norman inheritance. His role in life was to reinstate the dynasty, to reclaim the natural status of the Drews as landed gentry of noble birth. First, he had better find a wife to start his dynasty going again, and she was Frances Richardson, daughter of a Derbyshire cotton-mill owner. They had five children in their fine country mansion in Sussex, which might have been enough in terms of heirs but a mansion in Sussex was not really it. Julius had been born for greater things.

The target had to be Devon and, more specifically, Drewstaignton, obviously the ancestral home of the Drews, or Drewes as they now were. Julius commissioned Edward Lutyens to design him a castle, a proper Norman castle with a keep and everything, and they began building in 1911. Work was slow, not least because Julius insisted on Norman quality standards and methods in stone-masonry, and it got even slower when the Great War took most of the workforce away. As was the way in that war, many who went never came back, and that included Julius's eldest son, Adrian.

The stonework was finished in 1925 and the family moved into Castle Drogo in 1927. Julius, after a stroke in 1924, was never himself again and died in 1931.

The founder may have left early but the stores had kept on growing, reaching 500 branches by 1903. In 1924, the company bought its big rival Maypole Dairy, keeping that name and trading style, and in 1927 bought Sir Thomas Lipton's shares in his British business, a quarter having already gone to Van Den Berghs and Jurgens (later Unilever). In the 1960s, Home & Colonial was still a power in the land and, with Maypole, Lipton and others formed the imaginatively titled Allied Suppliers. Through various mergers and transformations, all those names disappeared from our high streets. Whatever is left may possibly be found somewhere inside Safeways, which is to say, Morrisons.

Courtesy of The National Trust, Castle Drogo is open to visitors every spring and autumn.

Halifax

The Birkbeck Building Society was begun in London in 1851 and continued in orthodox fashion for a few years, but started issuing cheque books in 1858. When a new manager took over, a Mr Francis Ravenscroft, it called itself the Birkbeck Bank. Under his super-vision, the already burgeoning deposit business, offering excellent rates of interest on deposit and current accounts, developed even further and a smart building suitable for a fine London bank was put up in Chancery Lane in 1902.

According to the official receiver, the Birkbeck Bank's failure was due to 'shrinkage of securities' and 'lack of banking experience'. He could have added persistent rumours about financial instability leading to a run on the bank in 1910, but the rumours were probably due to the aforesaid shrinkage, especially in the gilts market, plus the inexperience. Anyway, the Bank of England came to the rescue, paying ten shillings in the pound to all depositors, but that still wasn't enough. The Birkbeck was bust.

The goodwill, what there was of it, and the new premises were bought from the receiver by the London County & Westminster Bank, later part of the Royal Bank of Scotland, which obviously learned a lot from the whole thing.

Building societies were never meant to be banks when they were formed; quite the opposite. Banks were for those who already had houses, large ones, while the societies were for the poor and honest. And the early building societies were never there for long. They were small clubs with a limited membership of subscribers, who saved towards buying land and building houses on it for themselves. When that was achieved, the society was dissolved. The first such society was probably started in Birmingham in 1781, to build houses in Deritend, a very old part of Brum now usually thought of as Digbeth and famous for the Bird's Custard factory.

The building society idea caught on. One impetus was the Reform Act of 1832 which extended the vote to any man living in property worth £10 a year. More Acts of Parliament were passed to regulate the societies in 1834 and 1836, and by 1850 there were 2,000 and more, 'many of them,' to quote Sir Josiah Stamp, Director of the Bank of England, 'marked by glaring defects in their financial arrangements'.

It was at about this time that the notion of permanent building societies came about. The original savings club had developed into one in which some members were investors only, not wishing to build anything other than their nest eggs, while others were happy to borrow from the central pool to help them get their nests. The difference between the interest rate given to savers and the interest rate charged to borrowers paid for the administrative costs of the society. If membership were to be unlimited, large numbers of savers could be attracted, more good could be done with housing, and more of the difference would be available to pay costs, such as salaries.

In 1892, the Liberator Permanent Benefit Building Society in London was the largest in the country. It collapsed in spectacular fashion. To quote Sir Josiah again: '(The Liberator) had long ceased to perform normal building society functions. In the hands of Jabez Spencer Balfour its funds were applied without scruple to all kinds of speculative enterprises. The frauds excited public indignation and disgust.'

Mr Balfour had been gambling with savers' money in high-risk markets, and more legislation was passed to make sure that such a thing could never, ever happen again.

Meanwhile, in a pub in Halifax, a new building society had been formed, one which stuck to the principles – careful lending, secure investment, ownership by the members (mutualism) – for the benefit of ordinary local people wanting a decent house to live in. Another Halifax principle was growth, to be achieved by opening branches rather than by acquisition, and so successful was this policy that the Halifax Permanent Benefit Building and Investment Society was the biggest in the country by 1913, and it had yet to open a branch in Scotland or London.

There must have been something solid and trustworthy about the town's name, because the second biggest society was the Halifax Equitable. When the two merged in 1928, the result was five times the size of the next one down. Over the years, financial institutions from all over the world opened an office in Halifax, needing to be at the feet of this financial giant.

Everything was tickety-boo until the Building Societies Act of 1986 allowed building societies to start behaving like banks (see above). They issued cheque books and credit cards, bought up chains of estate agents (the Halifax recently sold their 218 estate agency offices for £1) and thought about demutualising. The first to do so was the Abbey National. The Halifax merged with the Leeds Permanent in 1995, demutualised as Halifax plc, then merged with the Bank of Scotland to become a set of initials. In fact, it disappeared entirely as a company in 2007, transferring all assets to the Bank of Scotland, so when Lloyds TSB bought HBOS in 2009, all they were getting from Halifax was a slogan and some rather good TV advertisements.

'Following the trend of all commercial and industrial construction, stores are being concentrated in larger units. The small shop on the street level continues to exist, and the modern designers of its façade, in both Europe and America, have taken full advantage of new materials, combinations of colours and tastes in composition.' This text is from the *Encyclopaedia Britannica* c. 1938. The photograph is from 1950s Britain, where new materials and tastes appear not to have arrived just yet.

Charles Henry Harrod

That he was born on the 16th of April 1799, at Lexden in Essex, and that he was the son of William and Thamar Harrod, are known facts. There is the possibility that he worked for a miller in Clacton but otherwise he doesn't surface in history until 1830, when he married Elizabeth Digby. Lexden, a village then, a suburb of Colchester now, is quite near Birch, where the Digbys lived and had their pork butchery.

The Harrods' first child, a boy, died in infancy, and they had a daughter who died of measles aged 4, but three more boys would make it to adulthood, one of whom would become a rather big cheese in the shopping world.

In 1834, Charles was selling tea from a shop in Whitechapel. By 1839 he was a tea wholesaler in Eastcheap, City of London, and had a hand in running a one-room grocery shop in the street that would become Brompton Road in Knightsbridge, then a rural village, though not a parish, largely known for its pure air and water and becoming vaguely fashionable. The Harrod family, not yet fashionable, moved in behind the grocery shop in 1853 for their health, and Charles sent two of his sons off to be apprenticed in the grocery trade with other firms. Elizabeth died in 1860 and father sold the business to number one son Charles Digby Harrod in 1861, allegedly for £500, payable in instalments. There was another grocery too, in Old Compton Street, of which another son, Henry Digby Harrod, became the owner.

That was it, really. Charles Henry lived long in retirement and died in 1885. It took just three years for Charles Digby to pay off father's £500, whereupon he married Caroline Godsmark, daughter of a grocer, perhaps the one with whom he'd been apprenticed, and over the years they would have seven daughters and a son. That he could pay his debt so soon, and set up in marriage, was through his pursuit of a novel policy. Like Jesse Boot, he decided to give no credit, which risked alienating the gentry moving into the new houses in the Brompton Road. Knightsbridge was fast becoming one of the most fashionable residential districts of the West End, but Harrod advertised cash only, low prices and free delivery, expecting to cater for 'The Peer and the peasant'.

There weren't all that many peasants in Knightsbridge by now, but if anyone was exceptionally hard up and couldn't afford essentials, Charles Harrod was known to charge purchases to his own account. He was benevolent to staff too, giving anyone who was taking a holiday a half sovereign. This was a time when prices were falling and wages were rising, so it's hard to say what a half sov, ten shillings, would have meant to someone such as a department manager on maybe £60 a year, or an assistant on £35 a year. Certainly it would represent at least £150 in modern money towards the cost of travel but rather more in gratitude from a sales girl unused to much luxury.

Charles was also unusual in paying overtime, but usual in fining staff who were late. He hosted an annual dinner with everyone there, and interviewed every new applicant for a job personally. Like John Spedan Lewis (*qv*) and Gordon Selfridge (*qv*) after him, he realised that customers bought the sales staff as much as the products, and so the quality of both were equally important.

In 1883 there were six departments in a much enlarged shop, with 200 staff on the books. Christmas of that year became a memorable occasion, because there was a huge fire on 6 December and everything burned. Harrod decamped to temporary premises and undertook that every order would be fulfilled from new stock, by Christmas. The publicity attached to his promising and achieving this extravagant aim probably did more for the Harrod image than anything else, and folk flocked to the opening of the magnificent new Harrod's store in 1884.

He was a recognisable fellow about the place – as we would say these days, high profile. Customers would ask to be served by him, he being so handsome and obliging, but his shop days were numbered. 'A man is as old as his arteries' was a well-known medical saying, and Charles's were hardening. He had arterio-sclerosis, often described as a disease of old age or intemperate living, but church-going, family man Charles, by no means in-temperate, was forced to retire aged only 48. Realising that partial retirement would not be enough, he sold out completely to a group of business people, who floated the company on the Stock Exchange.

Perhaps contrary to his own and the doctors' expectations, he lived a reasonably long retirement, becoming a Sunday school teacher, JP and county councillor, and died in 1905 aged 64.

Seemingly unable to follow such a good act, the newly-quoted business got off to a hesitant start, but then flourished and its directors, particularly the MD Richard Burbidge, were forever innovating. They installed the first escalator seen in a London shop. In 1906, Harrod's anticipated internet shopping by a century: 'Harrod's Ltd has made arrangements by which orders can be sent by telephone to them at any hour of day or night. It is thought that many persons find the ordinary business hours inconvenient, and to meet their requirements this firm have arranged to despatch orders received by telephone during the night by the first delivery next morning.'

Dickins & Jones, the *sanctum sanctorum* of drapery, was purchased in 1914, thus opening 'the door to the application of the Harrod method to that department of the retail industry' (*The Times* editorial). The much older firm of Swan & Edgar followed in 1920, with the largest window frontage (796 feet, over 240 metres) in London, which closed in 1982 to be replaced by a massive

CHAMPAGNE. (repeated down left and right margins)

HARROD'S STORES

(LIMITED),

BROMPTON-ROAD,

LONDON, S.W.

Telephone,
Nos. 542 and 845, Kensington.

Telegraphic Address :—
" Everything," London.

IMPORTANT SALE

OF

3,750 CASES HIGH-CLASS

CHAMPAGNE,

Prepared for the English Market, and Shipped in 1884, the corks
showing remarkably well.

We have secured a portion of the well-known Stock of

THE CAFÉ ROYAL,

Viz. :—

1,600 CASES QUARTS

and

500 CASES PINTS

of

THE SELECT BRAND,

JULES CAMUSET (estd. 1796),

" 1880 VINTAGE,"

WHICH WE OFFER AT 69s. PER DOZ. QUARTS.

(Pints, 5s. per two doz. extra.)

ALSO

450 CASES HAU ET CIE.,

GRAND VIN.

EXTRA BRUT "1880 VINTAGE,"

AT 60s. PER DOZ. QUARTS.

(Pints, 5s. per two doz. extra.)

We guarantee every bottle full and in perfect condition.
Delivered Free to any Railway Station in the United
Kingdom.

This is the image we associate more with Harrod's than cash trade with peasants. Anyone fancy a dozen quarts of vintage champagne at 60 shillings? So now we know, in 1897 high-class champers was half-a-crown per pint. Cases were delivered free to any railway station in Britain, and all bottles were guaranteed full, at prices 'hitherto unknown in the trade'. Please note the address for telegrams: 'Everything, London'. And we thought Whiteley was the Universal Provider, and Selfridge had 1 as his telephone number ...

In 1913, with war only a year away, ladies' fashion carried on regardless. This full page advertisement appeared in several national newspapers, which meant it was seen all around the Empire and elsewhere. With a Harrod's corset, the colonel's wife in India could take tiffin feeling that she was forever cast in the British mould.

'development'. D H Evans, founded in 1855, was taken over in 1928 and that great name disappeared in 1999 beneath House of Fraser 'branding' because it didn't inspire sufficient loyalty.

The Burbidge dynasty ran Harrod's until taken over by the House of Fraser in 1959. Mohamed Al Fayed bought it in 1986 and sold it in May 2010.

Joseph Hepworth

The man behind the name of Hepworth's Tailors was a Victorian who died just as Burton's and Price's were getting moving. At the age of 10, in 1844, he left his Huddersfield school to work half-time in a mill, then full-time, rising to overlooker by 1860, then taking to the road as a commercial traveller. Meanwhile he'd married Sarah and fathered the first few of their seven children. Sarah's brother James Rhodes was a tailor, and Joe Hepworth could get by in that trade too, so together they set up a small workshop in Briggate, Leeds, making up clothes for the wholesale trade.

Hepworth went solo in 1865, and by 1881 was employing 500 in a Wellington Street factory, including his son Norris. This was a bright lad, who pointed out their vulnerability while they relied entirely on the ups and downs of miscellaneous retailers. How much better it would be to own their own shops.

Many suits – and hats – on the beach at Scarborough in Edwardian times.

Whether Joseph Hepworth & Son was the first firm to take this step is debatable; certainly, the Hepworths were among the first and, equally certainly, they were the best at it. By 1890 they had 100 shops, considerable wealth and ventures in Australia and South Africa.

In 1906, Joseph was made Lord Mayor of Leeds, much to the consternation of some councillors and their wives because Joe was a strict Methodist teetotaller. His philosophy led him to be one of the earlier paternal employers, giving his workers good conditions and wages, but it also made him ban all alcohol from council functions while he was mayor.

In 1907 there were 145 shops and two factories, and success followed success. Joseph Hepworth died in 1911 and Norris followed in 1914, so neither lived to witness the 160th shop in 1917, which made the firm undisputed Number One in British men's clothing.

It is often the way that the true pioneer's successors lack his vision and innovatory abilities. They follow too closely the pioneer's path, unwilling to change something that has worked so well, so far. Hepworth's was overtaken by Burton's and Price's although remaining successful at the stuffier end of the market and chugging steadily onwards until it came under the leadership of one Terence Conran. In 1981, the women's clothing chain Kendall's was acquired and, before you could say Innovatory Retail Store Concept, the whole thing had been transformed into Next.

Gustav Jäger

'Jaeger is a luxury British brand renowned for designing stylish, innovative and superb quality womenswear, menswear and accessories. The cornerstones of all Jaeger's collections are its coats, tailoring and knitwear, the majority of which are made from luxurious yarns and natural fibres such as wool, cashmere, camel hair, silk and angora.'

So runs the marketing blurb of modern Jaeger, a firm with 140 shops in the UK and Europe, more in faraway places such as Chile and Korea, and concessions in various department stores. In fact, Jaeger was the first concessionaire in Selfridge's in the 1930s. If we leave aside the intriguing notions that a brand can design anything

Dr Gustav Jäger of Neuenstadt, 1832–1917, was a very clever chap but just ever so slightly bonkers.

and that cornerstones can be knitted, we may read more of the blurb, which goes on to state that Jaeger was 'founded 125 years ago'. This is quite right in the sense of the first shop, but quite wrong if you are looking at the principal idea that drove the German scientist Gustav Jäger (anglicised as Jaeger), although his idea is maintained to an extent in the phrase 'natural fibres such as wool'.

Had he been around today, Gustav would have been thought an eccentric professor, a slightly potty boffin who knew a great deal about his subject but sometimes had difficulty choosing the correct tree up which to bark. He was the son and grandson of ministers, and married the daughter of one, and himself set off for the pastorship but deviated into medicine and natural sciences instead. Later, he researched zoology, anatomy and anthropology, in the light of Darwin's new thinking – for which he was a great enthusiast – and taught these subjects at various German seats of learning.

Cerebral though he was, Gustav's health was not so good. He was unable to take sufficient exercise because of a bad leg and so looked into other ways he might heal himself. His studies of animals led him to believe that they, furry creatures all, were generally healthier than their human superiors. The beasts of the earth could stand out in the rain and the cold and never complain of any illness, while the naked apes, with God-given dominion over all living creatures that moveth, were forever sniffling and snuffling into their mustard baths and drinking senna tea, or cheap Epsom salts from Boots.

This state of affairs, he concluded, had to be because the beasts of the earth dressed entirely in natural fibres. He wrote a book about it. *Die Normalkleïdung als Gesundheitschutz: Mein System*, (roughly 'Protecting health with everyday clothes, my way') was published in 1880 and promoted the wearing of all-wool clothes, underwear as well as outerwear. Wool allowed the skin to breathe, it kept you evenly warm, and it insulated you against the cold draughts under the door, and thus would give you the same sort of rude health that sheep enjoyed.

The good Doktor obviously had never kept sheep, unlike your correspondent, or he would have known that they like nothing better than dying for no apparent reason. Also, curiously, Gustav did not extend his theory to the fowls of the air. Birds are seemingly as hardy as anything else but there was no recommendation from him that we should dress entirely in feathers.

Furthermore, cloth made from vegetable matter, such as cotton, should not be worn or slept in because it was not natural. Even your bedding should be all wool, so off with those fine Irish linen sheets and off with your silk pyjamas (silkworms did not qualify as hardy, healthy beasts). You, in your knitted nightie, will just have to get used to sleeping under the blankets. Quite what Gustav would have made of nylon, we can hardly imagine.

Mein System, said Jäger, had restored his own health and soon he had quite a following. He went on lecture tours and his doctrine gained ground among the Victorian chattering classes in Britain. One big fan, a grocer called Lewis Tomalin, with Dr Jäger's support set up a workshop to make all-wool, undyed, 100 per cent natural underwear, which in those days meant chemises, drawers and combinations (long johns plus vests), to be sold in a shop in Moor Lane, London.

How often these were washed would depend on the individual and those close to him or her, but it wasn't very often. This was a secondary issue, because Dr Jaeger's Sanitary Woollen System Co. Ltd was embraced by famous folk like Oscar Wilde and George Bernard Shaw. Little else was talked about in the salons and at dinner parties, although it was not much mentioned in the public bar of the Cat and Fiddle. Like Gulliver's Big Enders and Little Enders, the population divided into 'woolleners' and the rest.

Woolleners could go to the new shop in Regent's Street too, and twenty other shops. By 1914, the Doktor's name was being brandished about throughout the British Empire, but he didn't have much to do with the business directly. While enjoying the income from his licences, he became a practising physician in Stuttgart and died there in 1917, unremarked in the British press – not surprisingly, since we were at war with the Germans at the time.

The exhausted but hopeful world after the appalling disaster of the Great War, the war to end all wars, was not as interested as before in the distinguished, meritorious but rather dull house of Jaeger and its sanitary wares. A transformation was necessary, from clothing with a cause to clothing with a whistle. The route was by way of complete outfits rather than individual items. The notion was colours, designs and fabrics, all in one fashionable, co-ordinated look for the customer. The expression they used was: 'We don't sell clothes. We dress people.'

The kind of people they dressed remained upmarket, and the fashions were restrained and understated, using the finest cloth. Over the years, the name of Jaeger lost its double image of sensible woollen underwear mixed with a dotty philosophy, and moved

Here we have Jaeger's versions of John L Sullivan's eponymous lengthy garment. They may be hygienic, sanitary and natural, but are they quite the thing for dancing the Charleston?

smoothly and quietly into position as the arbiter of good taste, and by that, my dear, we mean English good taste.

After the Second World War, Jaeger became a little more adventurous in design and even began using some of these modern artificial fabrics, but there is only so far one can go without losing that, well, that Jaegerness. And quite right, too.

Jaeger Golfers, ideal garments for all sports – for steamer, river, seaside and country wear, the latest of the 21 styles of Golfers we are showing this season, supplied in 40 different shades.

Admittedly not on every high street – not all of them would be suitable, would they? – the Jaeger style, seen here soon after the Second World War, remains inimitable.

85

William Hesketh Lever

The man who brought you Sunlight, Vim and Lux began as a shop-keeper, in the family grocer's in Bolton, apprenticed at age 16 in 1867. He was a junior partner by 1872, went into manufacturing in 1885, made his fortune as the driving force behind Lever Brothers, and went back into shopkeeping in 1919 when he began buying up fishmongers all over the country.

With typical dynamism, he had about 400 shops within the year, the main purpose being to provide a large and secure market for 'his' fishermen, the fishers of Harris. His first intentions had been based on Lewis, and he bought the island, but he upset the crofters so much with his steamroller attitude that he sold that and bought the South Harris estate. Here he would build a kind of miniature Hull, with a great new harbour and a whole range of fish-processing facilities, and he would blast through to the inland loch and turn that into the haven of havens. Some of it was done, including piers and kipper sheds, and the tiny port of Obbe or An T-ob (Gaelic, simply enough 'the harbour') was renamed Leverburgh, whence now sails the ferry to North Uist.

The fish shops were all given the name MacFisheries, but Lever, or Lord Leverhulme as he had become, was suddenly not optimistic about fish in a world of tumbling prices, so he left the island as abruptly as he had arrived. He had to sell this personal project to his main operation, Lever Brothers, which didn't really want it, but it stayed there into the Unilever years. Lever died in 1925.

There was one major landing of fish at Leverburgh, in 1924 when twelve drifters from Great Yarmouth came in with the greatest quantity of herring anyone on the island had ever seen, but otherwise MacFisheries had to survive without its own source of supply. Although the name obviously implied that there was a direct link with Scottish providers, their buyers had to compete on the quays like anybody else. Rationing in the Second World War did them a big favour – meat was very strictly rationed, fish was not rationed at all. It was in short supply, fishing being a rather dangerous occupation with the Luftwaffe and the Kriegsmarine out to get you at every opportunity, but after the war, meat rationing continued. It finally came off ration in 1954, the nation rushed to the butcher's and MacFisheries felt the pinch.

Another blow came in the form of the frozen fish finger, so much easier to deal with than wet fish and, as customers began hurrying past to the new supermarkets, MacFisheries made their move. They already had a number of Food Centres offering groceries besides fish when they bought Premier Supermarkets from Express Dairies in 1964, and they added to that chain with new MacMarket stores.

"We 'are to take what fish we can get these days, Madam."

According to ex-MacFisheries shop manager Reg Joslyn, wartime fish supplies were erratic, to say the least. If there was any, they would put a notice in the window, 'Fish tomorrow, 10.30', and long queues would form hours before opening time.

Looks like Christmas is coming at MacFisheries, Cheltenham, in the 1930s. When did you last see a capon for sale on the high street?

With huge salmon and cod hanging up and all sorts of other fish, in Birchington, Kent in 1932, you are advised of 'Quality Always'. You are also instructed, mysteriously, to buy here or you are 'shopping weak'.

Sunlight *Soap*

"So Clean"

"So Clean"

(From the Painting by W. F. FRITH, R.A., Exhibited at the Royal Academy,
London, 1889, the property of the Proprietors of "SUNLIGHT SOAP.")

SIR CHARLES A. CAMERON, M.D.,

Ex-President of the Royal College of Surgeons. Chief Medical Officer of Health for Dublin, &c., REPORTS on "SUNLIGHT SOAP": "The points in the composition of this Soap that are most valuable are its freedom from free alkali, the large percentage of fatty acids which it contains, and the purity of the materials employed in its preparation. I EMPLOY THE SOAP, and from my actual experience of it can strongly recommend it.   (Signed) "CHARLES A. CAMERON."

The foundation of Lever Brothers, progenitor of Port Sunlight and the Lady Lever art gallery, was a bar of yellow soap. It was good soap, yes, but the genius was in the marketing. The name and the packaging gave it that special quality we now call branding. Before Lever had this idea, household soap was either home-made or bought in large lumps cut by the grocer from an enormous and anonymous block. He also introduced Lifebuoy, so he didn't have B.O., and he bought Pears, but he did not look a little lovelier each day with fabulous pink Camay. That was Proctor & Gamble. Nor did he have a schoolgirl complexion; Palmolive was made by an American called B J Johnson.

MacFisheries in Swindon, 1946, had cod fillet at a shilling a pound but it seems that the business to be in was bicycles.

Funnily enough, the long-standing connection with fish became a hindrance. Wet fish and other foods did not mix in the minds of the public, so the management cut the heads off the four fish on the logo. Some towns had a MacFisheries and a MacMarket. The main business of the parent company, Unilever, was in supplying MacMarket's competitors, such as Sainsbury and Tesco, and from 1975 they began closing shops that weren't making enough profit. In 1979, they sold the MacMarkets to International Stores and closed the rest of the fishmongers, and that was that.

John Lewis

Our first John Lewis in the line of succession that led to Waitrose, 'Never knowingly undersold' and parliamentary approval for MPs' domestic expenditure, was a cabinet-maker of Town Street, Shepton Mallet. He also tried his hand as a baker but his greatest success seems to have been in fathering children, starting with four daughters, then a son also called John in 1836, then four more

PETER ROBINSON'S
OXFORD ST.

THE BLOUSE
BEAUTIFUL.

No. 1
Fashionable Evening
Blouse, with Sequin
Berthe, Lined
Glacé Silk
In Black only
PRICE
35 9.

*

No. 2
Stylish
Semi-Blouse,
with handsome
Jet Yoke, &c.,
lined Silk.
In Black only.
PRICE **39 6.**

*

No. 3
Smart Dressy Blouse,
with Sequin Yoke,
trimmed Lace
In Black only.
PRICE **29 6.**

* *

Renowned for
RELIABLE FURS.

COSTUMES
FOR ALL OCCASIONS.

MANTLES,
GLOVES,
AND
HOSIERY.

A Visit is Respectfully
Solicited.

No. 1.

No. 2

No. 3.

Peter Robinson was one of the longest established names on Oxford Street. John Lewis had a job there as a buyer in the 1850s, when he would have been thinking about ladies in crinolines and flounces as shown by the illustration from a contemporary magazine (next page). In the 1890s, as can be seen from this advertisement, Peter Robinson's was renowned for reliable furs and offered costumes for all occasions to women who were a completely different shape from the way they are now.

infants, which effort exhausted his poor wife Elizabeth, née Speed. The father also died young, aged 45, leaving the orphans in the charge of various relations. Young John went to his aunt Ann Speed's, aged 6 with four more siblings behind him.

Times were difficult, yet somehow Aunt Ann managed to send the boy to the grammar school, whence he was apprenticed in Wells to a draper. Six years later in 1856, by a circuitous route, John Lewis was a buyer for Peter Robinson's (the ladies' outfitters bought by Burton's in 1946, kept going for years then rebranded as Topshop, now part of the Arcadia Group), in London's Oxford

Street, then lined mainly with small, individual shops and crafts-men's workshops.

John Lewis reached 28 years old and was still only an employee. This would not do. He rented one of those little shops for his own business in 1864 and began selling haberdashery and ribbons and bits and pieces, collectively known as notions, moving later into linens and other fabrics. He bought well, sold at reasonable prices, and worked very long hours, like Jesse Boot. Unlike Jesse, he had no great plans for expansion beyond the one street in the one city; just the same, it was a hard life for a hard-minded man.

After twenty years of it he'd made a deal of money. The 48-year-old John married the 30-year-old Eliza Baker, a schoolteacher from a Bridgwater draper's family and the following year, 1895, their first son was born. In the same year, John purchased Cavendish Buildings. The birth was to prove even more significant than the purchase.

Cavendish Buildings was on three floors, employing 150 people, of whom 100 were females living in a hostel nearby. In this shop, he was described as 'outfitter, upholsterer, furrier, a dealer in china, glass, cutlery, plate and ironmongery and an importer of oriental fabrics'; John Lewis now owned a department store. Nothing especially remarkable in that, but he was father to a revolutionary, of which more later.

He was something of a rebel himself, anyway, or perhaps we should call him a 'character'. He decided to buy Peter Jones of Chelsea; when the deal was struck, he walked to the meeting with the twenty grand in cash in his pocket, something like £8 million in our terms. He had a 23-year dispute with his freeholder, Lord Howard de Walden's Portland estate, during which he spent three weeks in Brixton prison for contempt of court, and exhibited potentially defamatory boards at the store referring to Lord de Walden's 'monument of iniquity'. His Lordship brought an action for libel and won, with damages of one farthing.

To *The Times* in 1913, John Lewis wrote: '... Hampstead is decidedly below even the modest level of efficiency which the telephone service actually maintains in other parts of London, a level which, I would venture to say, would not be tolerated in any private enterprise enjoying a monopoly and would mean speedy ruin to any undertaking in free competition. We live in an age when very grand hopes are widely entertained that State enterprise will prove a general deliverer from human ills.' Judging by the telephone service, it was Lewis's view that such hopes were doomed to fatal disappointment.

A couple of years on and he was in the news again. *The Times* reported: '... Mr Lewis had put up on a hoarding on his premises ... an anti-vaccination poster headed "Caution to Recruits". Mr. Cathcart (a Harley Street surgeon), noticing the poster as he passed by and regarding it as a hindrance to recruiting (for the Great War), obliterated it with his walking stick. Two men came up and remonstrated with him, and Mr Lewis himself attacked him from behind, knocking his hat over his head with an umbrella.' Lewis and Cathcart were both bound over to keep the peace.

These are indications of a personality that brooked no nonsense and, to his staff, this side of him often seemed excessive. He was brusque, intolerant, high-handed and, compared to some of our other high street heroes, mean. He had started with nothing like others but, instead of making him sympathetic to those with similar roots, his background made him all the more indifferent. He was the master; the workforce was his servant.

The servants went on strike in 1920, and Peter Jones was a mess, but still he wouldn't relinquish power to his sons, John Spedan and Oswald, both of whom had been taken into the partnership on their 21st birthdays. The old man died in 1928 aged 93. John Spedan Lewis bought out his brother, who went into politics, and took control. These are his own words:

> It was soon clear to me that my father's success had been due to his trying constantly to give very good value for money to people who wished to exchange money for his merchandise but it also became clear that the business would have grown further, and that my father's life would have been much happier, if he had done the same for those who wished to exchange their work for his money.

John the Younger looked at the accounts and saw that the profit, even in a business with poorly motivated workers and incompetent middle management, was equal to the entire wage bill. This great sum of profit had gone to father, which was far, far more money than he could ever want and of which he spent only a tiny percentage, while the employees were barely above the breadline.

John was not a socialist. He was a benevolent capitalist. Good business was the foundation of a nation's wealth. He said: 'There are too many public-spirited men in Parliament and elsewhere outside the world of business, and too few in positions of actual expert control of large industrial organisations.'

His great idea was that the relationship between employer and employee should be more like teacher and student, doctor and patient. This may sound condescending nowadays but it was seen

John Spedan Lewis was not a socialist, not a believer in democracy in business, but a revolutionary nevertheless, who set up a new kind of relationship between worker and boss.

as quite perverse proto-Bolshevism in some quarters. John thought that the very top brass, even the owners, should be content with a salary rather than limitless profits. Of course, profits were still needed to fund the business but any surplus above that required by prudent financial management should go to the workers.

The scheme he and his accountants devised was complex, involving trustees and so on, but basically it would amount to the employee being a shareholder, called a partner, in receipt of surplus profit in the form of shares that could be sold. In 1929, The John Lewis Partnership Ltd was formed, with just under 2,000 partners, including those working at Peter Jones.

Lewis believed in open communication, responsibility of managers to workers, efficiency, new ideas, and equality for women – one of his lady graduate recruits, Sarah Hunter, became his wife and deputy chairman – but he did not believe in democracy in business. He was the boss like his father before him and not entirely without his father's autocratic impatience, while being utterly dedicated to the improvement of the worker's lot.

He was a dynamic leader, not afraid to go where his father would never have gone, for instance buying a chain of ten grocer's shops in 1937 called Waitrose (originally Waite, Rose and Taylor, founded 1904). The first supermarket opened in 1955 as John Spedan retired as chairman of 12,000 partners.

John Spedan Lewis died in 1963. His idea was a brilliant one: he, as boss, believed that the bosses should limit their earnings so the workers could have more. Funnily enough, few have followed his line.

Thomas Johnstone Lipton

Born in Glasgow in 1850 according to himself, or in 1848 according to parish records, Thomas Lipton's parents were Irish immigrants with Scottish ancestry. Father, Thomas senior, a labourer back in County Monaghan, had various jobs in Glasgow before setting up in a small grocery shop in Crown Street, a busy residential and shopping street now part of the New Gorbals development. Ever an adventurous spirit, Thomas junior was only 14 (or 16) when he set sail for America, where he travelled widely, working his way on a tobacco plantation, another farm growing rice, as a salesman knocking on doors, and finally in a grocer's in New York where he took a close interest in American sales techniques.

He came home in 1870, helped out at his parents' shop then, frustrated by his father's lack of ambition, opened his own, Lipton's Irish Market, in Stobcross Street, Finnieston. By importing directly from Ireland he could undercut the competition and keep up high standards of quality. More shops followed, across Glasgow, then across Scotland and across the border. Like Jesse Boot, he understood the power of advertising and price-cutting stunts to keep his name in the public eye. One Christmas, he imported 'the world's largest cheese' from America, announced that it had gold and silver coins in it like a Christmas pudding, and watched as it was cheered through the streets from dock to shop where it sold out as fast as staff could cut it.

He always believed (again, like Boot) that to pile it high and sell it cheap for cash was a better route to success than that of the traditional grocer, selling expensively to upper-crust customers who wanted credit. By 1882, Lipton had shops in Paisley, Dundee, Edinburgh and Leeds and from then on, as he said, 'my only policy was to open a shop every week'.

He was being modest. Another policy came from his rebellious streak. He didn't see why he should conform to established methods of trading. For example, rather than buy his tea from wholesale importers in the London market, he went direct to source and bought tea plantations in Ceylon (now Sri Lanka), so he could sell at much lower prices than the competition.

His tea, 'from the tea garden to the tea pot', became a national institution, and an international one. He knew America, he wasn't at all nervous of it, and opened his packing company in New Jersey in 1893. Lipton's tea is a global brand today, although not so much in Britain where it began but familiar in eighty countries, according to Unilever, the owners at the time of writing.

It is said that he was a millionaire by the age of 30, a classification of wealth that hardly raises an eyebrow these days but then, for a Gorbals errand boy to amass such a fortune, in 1880 or thereabouts the modern equivalent of at least £100 million, was a noteworthy achievement indeed.

Queen Victoria dubbed him Sir Thomas in 1898 and he was made a baronet four years later. He never married and so the first baronetcy died with him in 1931, by which time he had long retired from business but not from society. He made five attempts on the biggest prize in yachting, the America's Cup, all failures, but he was host to kings, queens, princesses and presidents and among the most famous – and, we might say, best loved – men in the world.

Next time any reader hears one of the all-time favourite quiz questions: 'In what year was the first football World Cup held (and where, and who won it)?' the answer will probably be 1930 (and Uruguay, Uruguay), although you could argue for the 1920 Olympics, Belgium and Belgium. Of course, if you really want to upset the quizmaster, you could display your knowledge of a football tournament held in Italy in 1909. The prize was the Sir Thomas Lipton Cup, one of many he donated to sporting competitions all

This branch of Lipton's in Yorkshire seems to have gone in for ham and bacon in a big way. Smoked carcasses hang ready to be boned for the bacon slicer at eightpence ha'penny a pound. As with all grocers of the time, most foodstuffs were sold loose, that is, weighed to each customer's requirements. Here, huge cheeses await the attention of a person in a large apron with a cheesewire, while sugar is offered at three pounds (about a kilo and a third) for twopence. There's tea, tea and more tea, ditto margarine. One of the ladies in the picture would have been the cashier. As is still the case in 2011, in at least two butcher's shops, one in Sidmouth, Devon, one in Halesworth, Suffolk, the serving staff were not allowed to handle the money.

around the globe, and it was contested by a team of Turin, made up of players from Juventus and Torino FC; Sportfreunde Stuttgart of Germany; FC Winterthur from the Zürich Canton of Switzerland; and West Auckland FC of County Durham.

Why it was West Auckland's coal miners is not known for certain. We do know that the English FA refused Sir Thomas's invitation to nominate a team and that he insisted that a British team should take part. One story is that an Italian official mistook West Auckland for Woolwich Arsenal. Another, more likely, is that Sir Thomas delegated the matter to an employee who was a football referee, who then invited his favourite team from his own parish, the Northern League.

At any rate, West Auckland beat the Germans 2–0 in the semi and the Swiss 2–0 in the final. In 1911 the champions returned from Durham and again reached the final, to beat Juventus 6–1. According to Lipton stipulation, the trophy was now theirs to keep. Alas, the trips abroad had rendered them entirely skint. In fact, they were £40 down. Someone had the brilliant idea of mortgaging the trophy and persuaded the landlady of The Wheatsheaf pub to stump up. She kept the trophy for fifty years into her retirement, and relinquished it for £100 cash in 1960, whereupon it was put on show in the Eden Arms. Alas again, it was stolen in 1994 from its new home in the West Auckland Working Men's Club, and the cup now on show at that club is a replica. Still, the boys from the pit did win the real thing, the first World Cup.

Joseph Nathaniel Lyons

On 29 December 1847, in Kennington, Surrey, Hannah Lyons, née Cohen, presented her husband Nathaniel with a son. Prospects didn't look too bright for the boy. Father scraped a living, selling rubbishy jewellery and cheap watches around the poorer communities south of the River Thames and occasionally dealing in pictures. He never looked like getting anywhere, but maybe the boy would prove a godsend. He went to the nearest Jewish school, near Borough market, below Southwark bridge, and we might speculate whether that fine and ancient retailing institution had any effect on young Joseph, in view of the effect he was to have one day on the retailing institution we call the high street.

Borough market in about 1860, a place that Joe Lyons must have visited as a schoolboy and, presumably, one that left a firm impression on his business brain.

But no, young Joe set off in an entirely different direction. First he thought he'd be a writer, but everybody knew writing was a dodgy thing to do financially so he was apprenticed to an optician. He did his writing in his spare time – commercial novellas, mostly detective stories, and sketches for the music hall. He homed in on the Pavilion Theatre, Whitechapel as the hall of choice and while touting his wares there met the manager's daughter, Sarah Psyche Cohen, and married her in 1881. Joe was not a bad artist either; his watercolours were good enough to be exhibited and some were sold.

Still casting around for something that might make a rewarding career, he used the knowledge gained at the optician's practice to invent small optical devices, novelties really, that he could sell in numbers at the various exhibitions that were all the rage after the success of Prince Albert's Great Exhibition of 1851. At one such, in Liverpool in 1887, where he was charming people into buying his latest miracle gismo at a shilling, he was spotted by the principals of a tobacco firm, three men with an idea. They were thinking of going into catering and needed a front man, someone to test out the scheme without said principals being seen to be involved.

The three wise men were the brothers Isadore and Montague Gluckstein, and Barnett Salmon, and they thought it would be a wizard wheeze to have clean, tidy, pleasant little cafes at these exhibitions, where tired visitors could sit quietly with a pot of tea and a cake. Joe Lyons's mother was a relative of Isadore's fiancée, Joe himself obviously had the gift of the gab, so nothing could be more logical than to recruit the writer/inventor/artist with showbiz instincts to be mine host at the first cafe, or pavilion, at the forthcoming Newcastle exhibition.

It did very well, and was followed by Glasgow, Paris, Olympia and Crystal Palace, so the decision was taken to progress this simple service beyond the exhibitions and into the high street where, it was rightly felt, that same pot of tea in clean and pleasant surroundings would equally appeal to tired shoppers. We must remember that, while folk in twenty-first-century Britain expect there to be a Starbucks, a Costa and a Coffee Republic every 100 yards along the high street, nineteenth-century Britain had nothing of the sort.

To fund the venture, Salmon and the Glucksteins formed a public company, which they called J Lyons and Co. Ltd, making sure that their families had the controlling interest (which they were to keep until the 1980s) and appointing Joe as Chairman for Life. The first tea shop opened in Piccadilly in 1894 and was swiftly followed by many more across London.

The first Lyons Corner House opened in 1909, a vast restaurant on several floors employing hundreds of staff and feeding thousands every day. It also had a shop on the ground floor where Lyons tea, coffee, cakes and biscuits were on sale, and a Palm Court style orchestra playing most of the time. In the Corner House, as in the tea shops, the waitresses all wore a smart uniform in black and white. Initially known as Gladyses, they gradually morphed into Nippies, which name caught on to such an extent that it became the title of a musical, the name of a rose and a brand of cigarette.

There were actually only five Corner Houses, these multi-storey aircraft hangars of restaurants, but the name acquired much more currency because corner sites were always preferred for the hundreds of tea shops. Throughout the business, high standards of hygiene and service were rigorously applied; likewise quality

Wanda Hawley "Starring" for The Gaumont Co.Ltd in "Fires of Fate" & "Lights o' London"

writes:—

"I must confess to a certain discrimination in my choice of chocolates, and Lyons' are among the most delicious I have ever tasted."

"Delicious" is the word for Lyons' Chocolates. Made in over 80 varieties and each one more luscious than the last! Once they could only be obtained at Lyons' Restaurants and Teashops, but now leading Confectioners and Kinemas throughout the country sell them.

Always ask for

Maison Lyons Chocolates

and make sure!

4/- LB. Sold at Maison Lyons; Corner Houses, LYONS TEASHOPS and by most High Class Confectioners, Theatres and Cinemas.

Wanda Hawley, born 1895 in Pennsylvania as Selma Pittack, was a blonde, doe-eyed silent film star, as big a Hollywood name as Gloria Swanson. She played opposite Rudolph Valentino, Douglas Fairbanks and the other top leading men of the day, but Wanda was one of those beauties whose voice turned out to be a disaster when the talkies came along. *The Lights of London* and *Fires of Fate* were both silent pictures, made in 1923. Wanda may have confessed to a certain discrimination in her choice of chocolates, but did not extend the same characteristic elsewhere in her life and, reportedly, became a call girl.

in the pots of tea and the cakes, and the name J Lyons became synonymous with good value and jolly good tucker.

From there, the company expanded into all sorts of related activities, including hotels (starting with the Strand Palace), food manufacturing, ice cream (remember Lyons Maid? Mister Softee? Eldorado? Bertorelli?), more tea (Quick Brew, Horniman's), tea plantations, sweets, engineering works to look after the factories and a musicians department to look after the orchestras.

This expansion beyond the tea shops and corner houses mostly happened after Joe's death. He had been closely involved with the Territorial Army and various charities and was knighted for his public service in 1911. He was also Deputy Lieutenant of London County. He died in 1917.

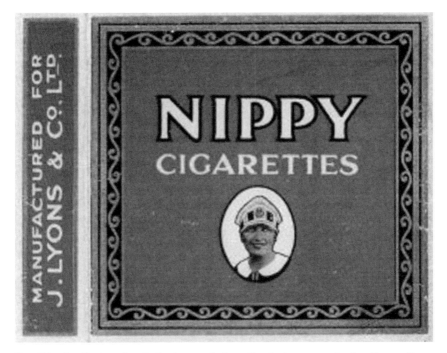

Possibly the first and only instance of cigarettes being named after the waitress who brought them to you.

After the Second World War, the company continued in dynamic style, for example employing a Miss Margaret Roberts, later Thatcher, as a research chemist, and opening the chains of Wimpy Bars, Golden Egg and Steak House restaurants, acquiring Dunkin' Donuts, Kunzle Cakes and Symington's, and building, in-house, the first business computer in the world. It was not the first electronic, stored program computer – Manchester University scientists had already built MUM1, and the US Census Bureau had theirs in 1951, the market for which was estimated at ten machines, but LEO (Lyons Electronic Office) was the first to run payroll and similar applications, and they built it themselves from scratch, with some advice from Cambridge University. Which was nice, until it was overtaken by a load of Americans called IBM.

Somewhere along the line, Lyons stopped shovelling the coal quite so hard and the steam ran down. Perhaps having the same families in charge for so long led to a certain complacency. In any

103

case, among the high interest rates and recessionary economics of the mid 1970s, Lyons found they were over-borrowed and struggling. In 1978, Allied Breweries bought the failing and sprawling empire of J Lyons and Co., still under the chairmanship of a family member, Neil Salmon, thus joining together in matrimony Tetley's beer and Tetley's tea. Allied Lyons kept the show going for a while but gradually sold off bits and pieces until there were none left apart from a few of the brand names.

Another well-known chain of cafes was begun by the Vey brothers as the Liverpool Coffee & India Tea Company in 1848. They opened shops all over the UK, plus one in Paris, changing the name to Mikado and then, by 1900, to Kardomah. The Swansea Kardomah became famous as the haunt of the Kardomah Boys, chief among whom was Dylan Thomas. In 1971, Kardomah was sold to Cadbury Schweppes and later to the American company Premier Brands, 'The world's leading tea company', where it is but the name on a tea packet. Kardomah cafes live on, in Swansea and elsewhere, now privately owned.

Michael Marks

It's a curious fact but the founder of one of the very best-known high street chains had little to do with the reasons why it became so. He may well have been born in 1859, certainly in the town of Slonim, now in Belarus, then in Russia. His mother died young, possibly giving birth to him. Widower Mordecai Marks was a tailor; his daughter looked after little Michael. Russian Jews did not enjoy many advantages in life and the anti-Semitic feeling was getting a good deal worse by the time Michael reached his twenties, so he left for England, for Leeds, with no money and no real idea of what he might do.

There was a well-developed Jewish social network in Leeds and this led him to a wholesaler called Isaac Dewhirst, who was sympathetic enough to lend him five pounds' worth of goods from stock. Michael's intention was to peddle the stuff around door-to-door but after some experience of that, he decided that a market stall appealed more. The market at Kirkgate in Leeds operated two days a week, so he did that and stood also at Castleford and Wakefield markets, and then moved into the covered market in Leeds.

It's an artist's impression long after the event, but you get the idea.

His slogan, 'Don't ask the price, it's a penny' caught on fast and he struggled to keep up with demand. Finding goods that he could sell for such a price, making a profit even if it was only a small one, meant he had to do the opposite of specialise. He bought anything and everything in his price range, from luggage labels to cotton reels to nails, and sold it as fast as he could get it, and was soon in a sufficiently financially stable position to ask Miss Hannah Cohen, a poor tailor's daughter, to marry him, which she did in 1886. As well as four daughters, they had a son, Simon, of whom more later.

Business boomed and Michael expanded into Lancashire, moving to Wigan and then to Manchester in 1894, where he opened his first shop and joined in partnership with Thomas Spencer, who had been Isaac Dewhirst's book-keeper for many years. Marks's retailing flair and Spencer's organisational and accounting skills proved a brilliant combination and in 1903 they made themselves a limited company. Spencer was happy that he'd done enough and earned enough, so he retired, and Michael Marks died in 1907 leaving a chain of sixty penny bazaars under central control and the name of Marks & Spencer, but no sign of the eventual legacy: 1,000 luxurious stores including 300 overseas, and a name that's known everywhere in the world where people wear jumpers.

After Michael's death, managers ran the show for a while. Simon Marks, son of an illiterate mother and a semi-literate father, went to Manchester Grammar School and studied abroad for two years. His school friend Israel Sieff married his eldest sister Rebecca, who became well-known for her feminist and Zionist activities, and Simon married Sieff's sister Miriam. After experience at head office, Simon became a director in 1911 at age 21 and chairman in 1916, after a legal battle with Spencer's executors. Brother-in-law Israel joined him as joint MD and deputy chairman and the two of them set about transforming M&S into a national treasure.

One major step was to miss out the wholesaler and deal directly with the manufacturer, in 1926 an unusual but not unique thing to do. What was novel was Simon Marks telling the manufacturer what to make and how to make it, and gradually moving to almost entirely British goods, all sold under M&S's own trademark name, St Michael, first used in 1928.

The two bosses also cut the range of goods drastically, as part of the chain's transformation from working-class jumble sale to all-class, high quality clothes retailer. The move into food began in 1931 but didn't really grip the nation until the 1970s, when they introduced sell-by dates, wine, ethnic exotica and refrigerated displays. They got Northern Foods to make them some fresh cream trifles and the rest isn't just history. It's M&S history.

Meshe David Osinsky

Many Russian Jews came to Leeds during the pogroms of the 1880s, so it might have seemed the obvious place to go for an ambitious lad from Kerkel, Kovno province (now Kaunas, Lithuania) who, aged 15, came to England in 1900. He didn't go to Leeds straight away, however, and instead earned his first crusts selling small items of clothing door-to-door in Manchester. A year later he was in Chesterfield, and two (or three) years after that he opened a draper's and hosier's shop there, with £100 borrowed from a relation.

There was no tailoring or drapery tradition in the family. Possibly young Meshe had spent those first Chesterfield years learning something about the craft but, more likely, he was studying the tangled precepts of business, especially retail business. His shop did sell suits, ready-made in standard sizes, but his main lines were shirts, stockings and caps, things that all working men wore.

106

Those off-the-peg suits were bought from a firm in Leeds called Zimmerman Brothers and they sold in the shop for about half of a poor man's weekly wage, an almost impossible sum for such a man because he had not a penny to spare. While the suit might be had for less than twelve shillings, the official poverty line was drawn at only ten shillings a week more than that.

Somehow, Meshe made enough money to convince his bank manager that he could cope with more. The bank was probably Beckett & Co., later to be subsumed into the London County & Westminster Bank, thence into the NatWest and Royal Bank of Scotland, to live on only as Beckett's Bank, a trendy wine bar in Leeds under the management of Messrs J D Wetherspoon.

More shops were opened in Mansfield and Sheffield, the latter very near one of Jesse Boot's first ventures away from home, and beside the Home & Colonial Stores. In 1909, Meshe married a Worksop girl, Sophia Amelia Marks, known as Cissie, by which time Meshe Osinsky was Morris (later Maurice) Burton. They lived in Sheffield but soon moved to Leeds where they, as partners in Burton & Burton, followed the Zimmermans into making off-the-peg suits for wholesaling. The differences were: one, they were following Hepworth's and so wholesaling to themselves and their own shops (by 1914 they had fourteen of them); and two, they also offered a bespoke service, applying the economies of factory tailoring to the personally fitted suit.

When war came, they naturally switched to forces' uniforms but still kept up the tailoring, by 1917 under the name of Montague Burton Limited. In the ten years after the war, Burton's went from forty shops to 400, meanwhile buying a factory on Hudson Road and developing it into the largest clothing works in the world.

All the shops were fitted out in the same way, more like banks than bazaars, with oak panelling, lush carpets and gunmetal fittings. The name of Burton, stylised in capital letters with that trademark curly B, shone above the windows against a marble background: Montague Burton, The Tailor of Taste.

With a close eye on the value of property, Burton liked premises that offered more options than just a tailor's shop, and many had rented offices, billiard halls or restaurants above. This was like a separate business and it was run personally by Burton from his house in Harrogate. He was authoritarian and non-delegatory enough in his tailoring activities. In his property dealings, he would let nobody in at all.

In 1931, little Meshe from Kerkel became Sir Montague Burton, not least because the financial success of his ever-expanding business was accompanied by a pioneering welfare system. Burton's factory had nurses, opticians, dental surgery, sick benefits clubs, sports grounds, and the largest works canteen in the world. The knighthood citation states 'for services to industrial relations'. They might also have said 'for services to the nation's standards of dress' for he, more than any other, brought the nicely tailored, smart suit within reach of the ordinary man in the street. As he himself said, 'A man's general bearing becomes more confident when he is well dressed'.

As well as suits, Burton was very important in men's leisure wear, by which we mean sports jacket, flannels and open-neck shirt. No thoughts then of jeans or T-shirts. The removal of the tie and the collar stud, and the replacement of leather shoes with tennis pumps, was informality enough.

In the late 1930s the Burtons bought a house down south, in Surrey, to be nearer the movers and shakers of business in London. When war came, uniforms were required, not in such numbers as in the first conflict, thank the Lord, but Burton's made something like a quarter of them.

When peace came, Burton had a small dabble in women's clothes with the purchase of Peter Robinson, but attention was much distracted when the weakness of sterling, plus market manipulation overseas, helped the price of imported wool to leap tenfold, twentyfold and eventually a hundredfold from 1945 to 1950. The wool in the cloth of a new Burton suit was costing far, far more than the suit itself. Of course, the wool price collapsed eventually and Burton's, unlike many in the trade, had been strong enough to ride the crisis. Things were looking up again by 1952, but The Tailor of Taste died in Leeds, giving an after-dinner speech in the Great Northern Hotel to his own senior staff.

He was a curious mixture, old Monty, frugal in his early days to the point of miserliness, yet hugely generous to his staff; something of a control freak, yet always telling his managers to live the business. The expression 'The full Monty', incidentally, may indeed be to do with our man. After the Second World War, men leaving the forces were given a mass-produced, off-the-peg civilian suit, called a demob (demobilisation) suit. Montague Burton's made many of these, mostly the standard two-piece but some were three-piece with waistcoat – the full Monty. Or it could be from men ordering a three-piece suit for a special occasion such as a wedding. There was an option in suit-buying to have, at a small extra cost, a waistcoat and a spare pair of trousers; perhaps it was that. Either way, you would ask in the shop for the full Monty. Or, it might be connected to the eponymous Field Marshal and his alleged habit of eating big breakfasts on campaign, or always wearing all his medals, or it might be to do with a Spanish card game called *Monte*, which is probably stretching things a bit far.

As to 'Gone for a Burton', widely used in the RAF in the Second World War to mean being shot down and killed, there are half a dozen explanations, one connected with a wartime aircrew wireless training school held upstairs in the Blackpool branch of Burton's. It is not clear quite how someone attending or perhaps failing the wireless course could be equated with one falling from the sky to his death. Surely, he would have been for a Burton, not gone for

Two Durham coalminers, with wives and suits, on a day trip to the seaside in about 1950.

one. Another story suggests a link with buying a suit for a funeral. Hmmm.

Whatever, the name lives on in our high streets, now part of Arcadia Group with Dorothy Perkins, Evans, Miss Selfridge, Topman, Topshop and Wallis.

Three suits for a wedding, 1947.

Henry Price

We're in Leeds again, because it's tailoring, and it's 1907. More precisely, we begin at Silsden, a small Airedale town between Skipton and Bingley, where a young man called Henry Price opened a men's outfitters. By 1928 he had seventy-four shops and the inevitable factory in Leeds, and by 1931 he had 112 shops and two factories in Leeds.

His approach was a little different to Burton's but, for a while, just as successful. Price's Tailors Ltd aimed firmly at the non-exclusive, cheaper end of the market. There were two main types of customer: one, the older working-class male who needed to replace his 'Sunday best', the suit and tie he wore for Sunday church, weddings and funerals; and two, more importantly, the young working-class male who had to have a suit and tie for pay-day/Friday/Saturday nights out. It must be remembered that nowadays when lads have a wide choice of casual clothing, affect a moderate interest in fashion and wear just about anything when out at the weekend, in the golden years of Burton, Price and the rest, most working men had just a few well-defined sets of clothes. They had whatever they wore at the job six days a week, and they had a suit, maybe they had a sports jacket and flannels, and they had the old, worn, patched remains of previous versions for the allotment and going to the match.

Your correspondent's father was a large policeman, and his working clothes were a uniform made of very stout material. Uniforms were replaced every so often, to maintain the policeman's smart appearance (yes, this was a long time ago). Used uniform trousers were shipped off to various members of mother's family, in whose households the menfolk worked down the pit or on the railways. These men were generally of average height or less, so there was plenty of scope for saving money by remaking this high-quality cloth into long-lasting work trousers. Regardless of what they looked like at work, these same men appeared every Sunday at chapel in a smart, clean, well-pressed suit, bought from one of the chains.

Price's slogan was 'The Fifty Shilling Tailors' – indeed, this was the name in large letters across the front of most of his shops. The remainder, perhaps trying to appear a little upmarket in slightly classier districts, called themselves John Collier, but all the suits

Sports jacket, flannels and blanco'd tennis shoes made the cool outfit for the young working-class male out on a spree in the 1930s.

were made in the same factories in Leeds. The cloth was not of the best, the cut and fit were adequate, but the fifty-bob suit was a hit.

Fifty shillings (two pounds and ten shillings) in the 1920s and 30s was the weekly wage for a lot of young men, so that's probably the best way to think about it as a modern equivalent. In those days, although the suits were made in factories, there was still a great deal of handwork. Today, when technology has largely replaced the factory workers, a 20-year-old can buy an off-the-peg suit for much less than his weekly wage – should he want to do so, and there was the rub for Henry Price's business.

Eventually there were seven factories employing 5,000 people, and 399 branches of John Collier/Fifty Shilling Tailors, including a good 100 that had been Stewart's bought on the way, and thirty-seven Claude Alexander in Scotland (not to be confused with Alexandre).

United Drapery Stores bought Price's in 1953, on the natural assumption that young working-class men would always want a suit and tie for Saturday night. UDS were not delighted by what they found in the upper echelons of Price's management and so, to beef things up, they dropped the Fifty Shilling name, changed it all to John Collier, and acquired the more upmarket Alexandre Tailors in 1954, eighty-eight shops.

Let us move on to 1967, when UDS had added Brooks Brothers and Peter Pell to the tailoring strength. It was still almost obligatory among young working-class males to wear a suit, white shirt and coloured tie, often red, for a Saturday night out, even if it was only at the pub. John Collier was selling two-thirds of its suits at less than £15 and none over £20. Alexandre sold two-thirds at over £15, with a quarter over £20. Collier's cheapest suit was £9 19s 6d. The difference in price between ready-to-wear and made-to-measure for an average suit was £1 7s 10d, let's say about £20 modern – or twice that, thus.

Using a straight comparison via the Retail Price Index, a suit at £14 19s 6d was the equivalent of £200 today. Bringing average earnings into it, that is, the ability to pay as a proportion of income, a proper price would be double, at over £400. Off-the-peg suits, as anyone can easily see by checking the internet, are very much cheaper now, whichever index you use. Even so, in 1967 UDS were making and selling well over a million suits a year. Burton's and Hepworth's were making even more.

At about this time, your correspondent's years at the University of Leeds coincided with the opening of the new hall of residence, the Henry Price Building. Like the rest of the 7,000 students then at

On a corner of Silver Street in Salisbury, one night in 1952, nothing happens outside the Fifty Shilling Tailor, Hepworth's, Bowyer's Wiltshire Bacon and MacFisheries.

114

this ancient seat of learning, he had no idea who Mr Price was and never gave that ignorance a second's thought. Although his own first suit had happened to come from Burton's, at about £14 in 1962 (ish), many of the other 6,999 must have had theirs from the Fifty Shilling Tailor. Certainly we could all sing the TV jingle, 'John Collier, John Collier, the window to watch'.

Then we had the dawning of the Age of Aquarius, flower power and other sorts of herbal power, Carnaby Street and the replacement of the dance hall with an entirely new kind of establishment, where you paid good money to hear somebody put a record on. Suits as Saturday night garb were on the decline. In 1985, Burton bought John Collier and soon the name disappeared altogether.

Joseph Arthur Rank

J Arthur's father was born in 1854, in a cottage by a windmill in Hull. He was a fervent believer in the survival of the fittest in business and in teetotal Wesleyan Methodism in his private life. This combination he passed on to his son but not in its entirety. Some of the nature, red in tooth and claw, was left out of J Arthur's make-up but Methodist, teetotaller and fine businessman he was all the same.

Joseph Arthur Rank, born in 1888, was bound for the milling trade but, instead of one windmill to attend to, by the outbreak of the Great War his father had built modern, mechanical mills in most of the major ports that were suitable, with power-driven metal rollers instead of millstones, and a huge trade going on. J Arthur left it to join up as a private soldier and served in an ambulance unit and the artillery, leaving the Army as a captain, to become a Sunday school teacher, the owner of the *Methodist Times*, still a miller, and managing director of Joseph Rank Limited when it was floated in 1933.

So far, all J Arthur had done for our high streets was fill the flour bins of large numbers of grocers. Now he took a turn which would have a rather more visible effect. Deeply disappointed by the moral quality of Hollywood films, which were most of what British audiences were seeing, and at the rubbish masquerading as religious films for children, he began the Religious Films Society.

His friends in the chapel and family thought he was mad to get involved with such devil's work as cinema, but he had a mission. His early films were too high-minded for the cinema owners, a frustration that decided J Arthur that he must have his own cinemas, starting in Leicester Square. To increase and better control production of films, he bought a mansion and turned it into Pinewood Studios, and then the Second World War began. Rank knew he had a patriotic as well as a religious duty.

He took over Odeon cinemas and Gaumont-British, including their 250 cinemas, and added Gainsborough and Ealing Studios. Really, after that, there was nobody else in the British film industry. J Arthur Rank was it.

Possibly his most famous wartime films were *In Which We Serve* and *Henry V* starring Laurence Olivier. There was *This Happy Breed*, and *The Way to the Stars*, and, after the war, *The Wicked Lady*. A highwaywoman as high-class tart was hardly J Arthur material but business was business, and he had 650 cinemas to fill. The Rank Organisation continued to fight the pernicious influence of Hollywood but government interference made a mess of things

The boxer Bombardier Billy Wells used to bang the gong before every Rank film, becoming stylised as a universally recognised trademark, still used by the Rank Group.

The Hollywood films of the 1930s were seen by J Arthur Rank as an immoral influence on the British people. He was going to put a stop to it.

and, despite triumphs such as *Great Expectations, The Red Shoes, Brief Encounter* and the Ealing comedies, it was very rough going indeed.

His brother died in 1952 so J Arthur had to return to milling. He left the Rank Organisation in capable hands and under various conditions which prevented an American takeover and ensured generous donations to charity. The Rank Organisation became Rank Xerox and the Rank Group (Butlin's for a while, and bingo), Joseph Rank became Rank Hovis McDougall plus Cerebos, and J Arthur became Sir J Arthur, Baron of Sutton Scotney, in 1957 and the main supporting pillar of British Methodism, with a sideline in gundogs and shooting on his country estate. He died in 1972, a year after his devout and supportive wife of fifty-four years, Laura Ellen Marshall.

In the 1980s, a holding company bought Lockwood's from the receiver. Readers of a certain age will remember Lockwood's tinned fruit and vegetables, similarly Smedley's and Morrell's, which were also acquired. Then there were Hartley's jam and Hayward's pickles, Chivers, Branston, Crosse & Blackwell, Sarson's, Oxo, Batchelor's, Homepride, Fray Bentos and, in 2007, what was now Premier Foods acquired RHM, Rank Hovis MacDougall, and with it Mr Kipling, Sharwood's and other household names.

So that's where J Arthur is now. Bearing in mind the broad acres of his birth, perhaps he wouldn't have minded ending up in a group with Hammond's Yorkshire Relish.

Harriet Samuel

Yes, most people would assume that the H in H Samuel stood for Harold or possibly Horatio or Havilah, but it doesn't, although it very nearly stood for Henry. As it is, the initial is for the good lady Harriet, née Shriener Wolfe, who married Walter Samuel, second son of Moses Samuel, a clock-maker and silversmith of Liverpool. Moses died in 1860, leaving the business, £59 10s and fourteen lever movements to Walter, cutting out number one son Henry (who, incidentally, had married Harriet's sister, Rachel).

In his will, the old man pointed out that Walter had looked after him in his declining years. He did not mention Harriet but we can assume that she had most of the burden to carry, when she and Walter had father Moses living with them. The elder boy Henry contested the will, probably anxious to get hold of some of the £59 10s (think £40,000 in today's terms) but made no progress.

It must have looked like matters would go Henry's way in any case, as Walter's health was not so good. If Henry harboured such thoughts, he reckoned without the redoubtable Harriet, who began taking more of the decisions, one of which was to start using the name H Samuel in 1862. Walter died in 1863, so Harriet was now the boss. She was no watchmaker but, my oh my, she understood sales and marketing all right. Also, she wanted a fresh start, away from all the family ties and history in Liverpool, so she moved the business to Manchester, to No. 97 Market Street, then a real street and part of the old London-to-Carlisle road, later classified as the A6, not a pedestrianised precinct running beside an Arndale Centre. There, she set about developing mail orders from press advertising as her prime strategy.

Here's some of the text from one of her ads, in the London *Penny Illustrated*, 1884:

H. Samuel's unrivalled and world-famed watches are universally acknowledged to be without equal, combining the best workmanship, the most superb appearance, the highest intrinsic value, and are supplied at the wholesale price, being therefore the greatest boon ever offered to the public.

Clearly, our Harriet had a way with words. Her watches, said to retail at £5 5s, are offered in the ad at only £2 12s 6d and are *the marvel of the age, the delight of many thousands of their possessors, the most accurate time-keeper in the world; in fact, paragons of perfection.*

You are asked to beware of imitations. *Buy direct from the Lever Watch Factory, Manchester, and you will have an unending source of gratification.*

Interestingly, in an age when nobody would have expected to find a mere woman behind such an enterprise, Harriet wrote: *H. Samuel's name has become world-famous from the unvarying excellence of the Watches supplied by him.*

Her son Edgar was more interested in the retail side than mail order, and opened a new store in Preston in 1890, and one in Rochdale. Soon, there were branches all over Lancashire and further east and south.

Harriet died aged 72 in 1904. The centre of the rapidly expanding retail business was moving south and Birmingham seemed the logical place to be, so the HQ was moved there in 1912. After the Second World War, H Samuel and her 'Everite' watches (made in Switzerland) grew to 200 shops and, by acquiring James Walker, the London-based chain of jewellers, to almost double that.

Now, H Samuel is part of Signet, an American-owned firm with over 550 branches in the UK (including Ernest Jones) and 1,400 in the USA.

Harry Gordon Selfridge

By no means a name in every town – very few, in fact – Selfridge is a high street hero nevertheless. His style and methods in his main department store, in Oxford Street, London, were a great influence on British retailing and, if you ever wanted to shoot the person who coined the phrase 'Only X shopping days to Christmas', you're too late. Harry Gordon Selfridge died in 1947.

He was a dynamic fellow who admired the finer things in life and loved excitement, a combination of personality factors that would prove his downfall eventually, but the young Gordon had no thought of such a fate. His father Robert, a soldier in the American Civil War, had had a small shop in Ripon, Wisconsin but he never came back from the war even though he lived through it, as a major in the Union cavalry. Gordon's mother Lois brought him up in Jackson, Michigan, earning the family bread as a schoolmistress. The boy wanted to be a naval officer but couldn't pass the physical, so he joined a bank as a junior clerk and, after five years of that, took another clerical post but this time with a department store in Chicago called Field, Leiter and Co., which eventually became Macy's.

Young Selfridge soon got himself onto the sales floor and was manager of the store in six years, became a junior partner in the firm, and married a Chicago society girl, Rosalie Buckingham. Trips abroad, especially the ones to Paris and London, convinced him that New World methods would be a hit in more civilised but less up-to-date regions, and he tried to persuade his colleagues at

Field, Leiter that they should open a store together in London, then the greatest city in the world. Failing to get their commitment, he retired aged 39 with a considerable fortune, and moved to London. Retirement didn't suit, although he threw plenty of energy and money into his social life, and so he began planning a new store on a grand scale.

He had an American architect to design the building, for a site on Oxford Street, and brought over his window-dresser from Chicago days to amaze those conservative London shoppers. There were 130 different departments, plus customer services both expected and unexpected. Restaurants, yes, even one offering southern fried chicken and corned beef hash; a library, yes, and rest rooms; these were reasonably conventional and designed to keep people in the store for longer – but cricket bat oiling and wart removal? Such things were largely unknown in the British retail industry but, above all, to go with these extra services, there was a new kind of staff training.

The problem the British had with service, and still have to some extent, was that it was thought in some way to be demeaning. Historically, retailers had concentrated on the high-value,

"How is it I never get what I ask for in this shop?"
"Because if you did, I should get the sack!"

Another phrase that Gordon Selfridge is supposed to have coined: 'The customer is always right.'

high-profit kinds of product aimed at the upper ends of the market, which had produced a master-servant relationship between customer and shopkeeper, and so to be 'in trade' was considered a social black mark. Sir Thomas Lipton, for example, rich as he was and despite his friendship with kings and despite his America's Cup adventures, was turned down for membership of the Royal Yacht Squadron basically because he was a grocer and was only admitted very near the end of his life.

Americans had no such prejudices. Americans saw service as part of the product. Gordon Selfridge looked around London and saw shops where customers treated the sales staff as mere fetchers and carriers, while the sales staff smiled and kowtowed and quietly hoped their customers would burn in hell. Gordon's idea was to train staff to be helpful, to advise, and to sell. In return, he expected customers to start thinking of shopping as a leisure activity. Of course, the customer was still always right but, with the professional help of trained sales staff, the customer would be right a lot more often.

After Harrod's, Selfridge's was the biggest store in London, with about 6 acres of sales floor. Window displays, extravagant advertising, stunts such as putting M Blériot's aircraft on display the day after he crossed the Channel in it, and a generally flamboyant, larger-than-life way of doing things kept Gordon and his shop well in the public eye for years, even through the Great War, but against some powers even the great, top-hatted Gordon could not prevail. As the war ended, an influenza pandemic swept Europe. Among the millions carried off by 'Spanish flu' was Mrs Rosalie Selfridge.

Gordon's reaction, if that's what it was, would end in tears and penury. Always the man to think big, he began his new career as widower/Casanova with one of the King of Portugal's ex-mistresses, the actress Gaby Deslys, and bought her a house at which he could visit. The high-society interior designer and wife of W Somerset Maugham, Syrie (daughter of Dr Barnardo), was another who fell for his American chat-up lines.

In 1926 he met the Dolly Sisters, twins from Hungary, a vaudeville act with the Ziegfeld Follies and on their own, beautiful and glamorous, who sang and danced and used every milligram of their natural assets to achieve fame and glory. Some of their publicity photographs were beyond daring for the day. Men grew weak and breathless at the very thought of them. To have been given a smile and a shimmering glance from either Rosie or Jenny would have been enough to make most chaps happy for life, but Gordon Selfridge had these nightingales sing at his palatial home by Berkeley Square, and took them both to his bed – although not, we believe, at the same time.

He also took them, and others, to French seaside resorts with large casinos. In between buying Whiteley's (*qv*), to his great cost, and pushing a 1930s expansion programme in defiance of the economic climate, Gordon went on an eight-year fling. With the help of numerous actresses and casino owners, he ran through all his money and put himself, through the shop, heavily in debt. The other directors gave him a choice: pay back the money you owe, or resign on a modest salary. He chose the latter course.

Harry Gordon Selfridge died in 1947 with only a few thousand pounds to his name, at a small house in Putney Heath where he lived with his daughter, also called Rosalie.

In 1951 the ship was heading for the rocks but Lewis's, under the chairmanship of Lord Woolton, he of wartime pie fame, bought it, then in 1965 Charles Clore's Sears Group bought a controlling interest in Lewis's; Selfridge's was then demerged from Sears in 1998, the year that the new store was opened at the Trafford Centre outside Manchester. More spectacular new stores were opened in central Manchester and Birmingham and in 2003 the Canadian entrepreneur Galen Weston bought Selfridge's and, at the time of writing, still has it.

H W Smith

> *When I was a lad I served a term*
> *As office boy to an attorney's firm.*
> *I cleaned the windows and I swept the floor*
> *And I polished up the handle of the big front door.*
> *I polished up that handle so carefullee*
> *That now I am the ruler of the Queen's Navee.*

The audiences flocking to see the original production of Gilbert and Sullivan's *HMS Pinafore* would certainly have understood the satirical intent behind the words to this song. The character who sings it, Sir Joseph Porter, First Lord of the Admiralty, adds:

> *Of legal knowledge I acquired such a grip*
> *That they took me into the partnership.*
> *And that junior partnership, I ween,*
> *Was the only ship that I ever had seen.*

Some years before, in 1868, the highly successful and far-seeing businessman William Henry Smith II had become a Tory MP and, in 1874, Disraeli made him a Treasury minister. Of Treasury matters he acquired such a grip that in 1877 Disraeli promoted him to First Lord of the Admiralty, and in 1878 *HMS Pinafore* was performed for the first time.

W H Smith had never been an office boy in a law firm but the point remained. What he had achieved, however, was remarkable in itself.

It all started in 1792 with his grandfather, Henry Walton Smith, and grandmother Anna, who opened a small newsagent's in Little Grosvenor Street, London (now Broadbent Street W1), with a distribution network in the form of the man himself, H W Smith, paperboy. These were difficult times, but newsworthy. The French revolution was in full flow, the guillotine was popping heads into baskets like shelling peas, and the British government was looking under every bed for signs of the same thing happening in the green and pleasant.

Main sources of news for the folk of London were *The Tatler*, *The Spectator*, *The Morning Chronicle*, *The Morning Post* and *The London Gazette*. *The Times* was yet to appear. Tax, production costs and the limits of literacy meant that newspapers were bought only by the middle and upper classes, which is presumably why Henry and Anna set up where they did, in a wealthy area. Basing the price of a paper on the average earnings of the day, the tuppence (half of it stamp duty) you would pay Henry in 1792 meant that he was asking you to part with the equivalent of about £9 in today's money. No wonder he thought Grosvenor Square the place to be.

Alas, his health failed and he was dead only a few months after he got under way. Anna, a widow with three children, carried on without him but with a business associate called Zaccheus Coates, who died in 1812. News then was still a commodity of enormous interest. We had had Nelson's sea battles but the Napoleonic wars were not over, and we were at war with our ex-colonies in America. Anna and Henry's son William Henry was the likeliest lad for business; with his brother Henry Edward (lots of Henrys), he set about learning the trade. Mother died in 1816, the boys branched out into stationery and, with William clearly the dominant force, the business became W H Smith in 1828.

W H watched the growth of the railways with great interest and saw the possibilities for national expansion, using this entirely new mode of transport. His main trade was in distributing the London-based papers nationally, by road, but more quickly than the Royal Mail's overnight coaches. When Euston station opened in 1837, terminus of the London and Birmingham Railway, he seized the opportunity. Just as the motorway network and refrigerated transport made possible national food distribution, and therefore our supermarket chains, so the railways did the same for the vendors of less perishable goods.

W H's son, also William Henry, had expressed a wish to become a clergyman but his father instead set him to work in the business at age 16. He acquired a grip too and by age 21 he had been taken into the partnership. In 1848, W H Smith & Son tendered for the bookstall contract at Euston and, later, the other stations used by the now much enlarged London & North Western Railway. Station bookstalls had previously been a local matter, usually run by the town's newsagent, and the Smiths were rather late into it. William Marshall (later part of Menzies) had been at Fenchurch Street station since 1841 but couldn't match W H Smith & Son's offer of £1,500 per annum for the twenty-one LNWR stations. Passengers could buy books to while away the journey, usually the cheap editions at a shilling, or they could pay a penny and read their book while they waited for the train or, for a penny farthing, they could take a book on the train and return it at the Smith's bookstall on the platform at their destination.

The significance of this deal could not have been fully appreciated, even by the forward-thinking Smiths. At the stroke of a quill pen, W H Smith became the first retail multiple, not by opening one branch at a time as tailors and grocers did later on, but all at once. Suddenly, the Smiths had a national company with managers and employees in London, Liverpool and Manchester and all stops in between. This was a complete novelty at the time but they immediately did another deal, with the Derby-based Midland Railway, and they went on to tackle the whole railway business to such effect that by 1870, those twenty-one shops had become 290. More and more followed, plus wholesale newspaper depots in Birmingham, Liverpool, Manchester and Dublin. From the railway stations, papers were delivered far and wide, using handcarts, bicycles (150 WHS specials) and innumerable horse-drawn carts. By 1902, WHS had over 1,000 railway station bookstalls.

As if that were not enough pioneering for the man who would rule the Queen's Navee, he also had the idea of renting walls in the stations, on which to plaster large advertisements. Doubtless somebody else would have thought of it eventually but, as it happened, we have W H to thank for billboards.

Little did the citizens of New York know, but they had W H Smith to thank for the idea of outdoor advertising. On this high street, the neon is twelve storeys high.

126

A typical smaller station bookstall in 1956, at Cullercoats. The distinctive lettering of the name was designed by the great typographer Eric Gill in 1902. Rowntree's Motoring Milk Chocolate is sixpence a bar, and Woodbines are 'smoked by millions' including, we are surprised to learn, young lady tennis players.

The business continued to thrive after the deaths of the two W Hs and all went swimmingly until 1905 when something unforeseen occurred that would change British shopping for ever.

You could argue that Smith's railway bookstalls were the first chain store in the world, but they weren't on the high street. Jesse Boot had high street shops in Nottingham, Lincoln and Sheffield by 1884, and ten shops by 1890, so you could say he was the first; or Thomas Lipton with half a dozen shops in Scotland and one in Leeds by 1882; but that something unforeseen for W H Smith was also something really dramatic.

The railway companies announced that they wanted more rent out of W H Smith, and Smith's didn't want to pay it. The dispute resulted in contracts lost with the Great Western and the London & North Western railways. LNWR gave theirs to Wymans, later part of Menzies. W H Smith bought John Menzies in 1998, so it was only ninety-odd years that Euston was missing from the portfolio, and 150 years since it opened.

Smith's directors had, of course, been aware of the proverb warning of the dangers of putting all one's eggs in one basket, just as the railway companies had been aware of the pressure they could exert on such a one-basket company. As the new century turned, W H Smith high street branches had been opened in Clacton and Gosport, to go with the ones they were already operating, from years before, in Torquay and Pembroke Dock. Southport and Paris followed in 1903, then Scarborough, Leicester, Reading and Birmingham. Sixteen more were opened in 1905, and then the LNWR/GWR blow fell.

Smith's had got up as far as 1,250 station bookstalls. Now they were back down to 1,000 and the 250 gone included some of the biggest and best. Should they cut back, or should they go for it? In less than three months, the company set up 144 shops in towns from whose railway stations they had been evicted.

With panic over and dust settled, W H Smith embarked on a steady and considered expansion, always broadening the range of products and services, and gradually became a national institution. By the 1930s, people expected there to be a W H Smith wherever they happened to be, but from the 1950s on, changes were afoot that required a modern approach. Smith's moved to self-selection by customers, replaced sheet music with gramophone records, closed down the libraries (started in 1858), created the ISBN book classification system, moved into airports and the new shopping centres, swallowed seventy post offices and, in a logical development of William Henry's vision, set up their stalls in over 100 motorway service stations.

Both these bookstalls opposite were photographed in 1949. The dramatic experimental design of the Marylebone shop contrasts sharply with the traditional one at Victoria. The 'egg' WHS emblem on the Victoria stall, designed by R P Gossop in 1905, is a very early example of corporate identity, one we have more recently learned to call a logo (from logotype, a printing term from hot-metal days, for a word cast as one piece). Now every business has to be known by a set of initials. The Hong Kong & Shanghai Banking Corporation is HSBC, Imperial Chemical Industries is ICI, and we await with interest the press release from the marketing director of Xanadu Yorkshire Zithers Ltd.

Another emblem, the Septimus Scott newsboy which was usually a hanging sign, is modernised and made into plaques for the Marylebone stand.

W H Smith high street store with circulating library, parquet floor and oak furniture, at Northwood Hills, London, 1935.

And they say nostalgia isn't what it used to be. Just look at this shop front in Filey where, we are sorry to say, there is a Smith's branch no more. Note the egg logo in mosaic as you walk in, the gas lamps above, and the special section of fascinating books for boys and girls. The only thing missing is the WHS porcelain dog's drinking bowl. The photograph was taken in wartime, hence the rather subdued window display, but that style of front was universal until the Great Modernisation in the 1970s.

Joshua Tetley

Pubs are as much a part of the high street as banks, cafes and Boots, and there are many old beer barons who could be hailed as high street heroes. One will suffice, for his story and legacy are typical.

The boy was born in 1778, son of William and Elizabeth. William, like his father before him, was in the malting trade, and so he was badly affected when grain prices began shooting up in 1797 as a result of the Europe-wide wars with the French under General Bonaparte. Young Joshua looked on at age 22 when his father was declared bankrupt in 1800, but were they downhearted? No, because Josh, two of his brothers and father rebuilt the business, adding wine and spirits trading to the maltings in Armley and opening an office in London.

In 1808 Joshua married into the Leeds aristocracy, the families of the cloth, in this case the Carbutts in the person of Hannah Carbutt, and by 1814 they were living in Park Square, about as posh as you could get in Leeds then, with their five daughters.

At this time, it was much more common for a pub to brew its own beer than for it to sell beer from a brewery and, because of relatively high duty to pay for the war, you might say supply did not meet potential demand. Possibly Joshua Tetley spotted this, because in 1822 he took a lease on a brewery in Salem Place, on the south side of the River Aire. His investment paid off in diamonds and rubies when the Tory government, under Prime Minister the Duke of Wellington, took duty off beer and liberalised the licensing laws.

The result of the 1830 Beer Act was a boom in beer. Alehouses opened in nearly every street, almost all run by people who had no intention of learning to be brewers. They bought from people like Joshua Tetley and, ten years later, Tetley's was making a profit of £3,000 a year, which gave Joshua, now in his 60s, the modern equivalent of an annual income of £2 million. Soon, his personal wealth was ten times that. He'd already moved to the sweet air and parkland of Woodhouse after living at his brewery for some time, but now he did what so many wealthy Yorkshire people do. He moved to Harrogate, where the H is always pronounced.

In 1853, he passed control to his only son Francis, and died in 1859. Francis built a large new brewery and began exporting Leeds beer all over the country, even to Manchester, on the new railway system. By 1875 the beer boom was more or less over but Tetley's, at nearly 200,000 barrels per annum, was the biggest of the northern brewers. Francis's brewing life was also over, and he retired due to ill health and departed for warmer climes. He died in Bournemouth in 1883, having multiplied that £30,000 of personal wealth another ten times, leaving £300,000 in his will.

Wife Isabella had produced fourteen children in twenty-five years, seven of each, including son Charles who took over from father at the brewery. As befitted the son of a wealthy brewer, as opposed to the son of a bankrupt maltster that his grandfather had been, Charles was educated at Harrow and Trinity College and married the daughter of a solicitor. He became Lord Mayor of Leeds and a big sponsor of the university.

It was this Tetley who was largely responsible for building up their huge tied estate of pubs. Until 1890, they hadn't had a single pub. There had been no need but, as the business changed and so many of the alehouses closed, brewers saw the advantages of a guaranteed outlet for their products which, in Tetley's case anyway, were generally acknowledged to be excellent.

Next was Charles Harold Tetley who followed a similar route through Harrow and Trinity, but added a DSO for his bravery in the First World War. He was chairman until 1953 and died in 1959, just before the string of events that would lead to the disappearance of the world as he knew it.

Tetley's merged with the Warrington brewers Walker Cairns in 1960 to form Tetley Walker, merging again almost immediately with Ind Coope and Ansells to make Allied Breweries in 1961. Soon after that, one of Tetley's most loyal and enthusiastic customers, your correspondent, was lucky enough to gain a place at the University of Leeds.

Tetley's bitter was paler in colour than it is now, and much more bitter. It was a highly distinctive brew, quite different from local rivals such as John Smith's, Sam Smith's, Webster's and Cameron's. It was definitely an acquired taste. It was said that you could tell the age of any man in a Leeds pub by what he was drinking. If it was mild, he was over 40, having had to change from the much more challenging bitter in his middle age.

Moving to London, your correspondent, despite dedicated experimentation, took some time to acclimatise to Courage, Watney's and Charrington's, although heartily pleased to find Young's of Wandsworth, a similarly rewarding and breathtaking bitter, and Fuller's of Chiswick. Alas, the only Tetley's pub in London, the Rising Sun between King's Cross and Euston, where the British Library now is, could only illustrate what we all knew, that Tetley's didn't travel well. It was probably the infamous 'Warrington Tetley's' anyway; a brownish brew notorious for its poor showing against the golden nectar of Leeds.

Allied Breweries had national ambitions. They wanted Tetley's to be a recognisable brand beyond Yorkshire, like Coca Cola, and for that to happen the local character of the beer would have to be brewed out. It is an essential feature of a nationally drunk beer that

The Britons Protection, a famous Victorian pub in Manchester, largely unaltered from its origins, is one of the most visited pubs in the region. While other pubs have been refurbished, modernised, knocked into one room and closed, The Britons and its like remain the same, and crowded. It even has its old Tetley sign outside, which you might think had escaped the notice of the marketing whizz kids at Carlsberg. But no. They're bringing him back, on pump clips and so on, because 'The huntsman is at the heart of what Tetley's cask ale is all about'. Thus spaketh the top whizz kid while closing the brewery.

133

it offends nobody, and so gradually the bitter changed, to a darker, sweeter, blander, less assertive taste.

Everyone at the time was switching to pasteurised beer dispensed by carbon dioxide, but Tetley's didn't, and they were vindicated when such top-pressure beer and keg beer went on the wane, to be replaced by lager. Allied Breweries became Allied Lyons in 1978, which was bought by Carlsberg in 1998 to make Carlsberg Tetley, then the name of Tetley was dropped, and now the Leeds brewery is to close and production of the once legendary Tetley's bitter is to be transferred to Northampton, a place famous for making shoes. The announcement of the closure was made very quietly, the day after Barack Obama won the presidential election.

At the time of writing, real ale, or cask beer, is the only growth sector in the market, and Tetley, despite being the source of so much junk beer called smoothflow, is also the UK's biggest producer of cask beer. Your correspondent, weeping into his pint of Adnams, wonders how it is possible that the Leeds brewery can be closed, when it used to make one of the finest beers ever, ever brewed.

John Walker and the Rochdale Pioneers

In the National Library of Scotland is an old notebook and a deed signed by a few working men. Both date from 1761, and establish the founding of the first formal co-op on 14 March of that year. The co-op was called 'The Society of Weavers in Finnick', which we know as Fenwick in Ayrshire, not far from Kilmarnock. The weavers were hand-loom operators, of course, making tweed and muslin, self-employed men depending on merchants in town for work and payment.

The merchant and landowning classes did not like the idea of workers joining together in any way, to discuss politics or routes to self-improvement, but Fenwick had a bit of history in rebellion, having been a stronghold of the Covenanters, a Protestant religious group that held God as the head of the Church of Scotland, not the king. When the weavers, fifteen of them, signed their deed, they were probably thinking no further than their weaving livelihood, wanting to form a sort of trade association or union. It had to be done in secret, as such a grouping would never have been tolerated by the authorities.

Anyway, by 1769 certainly, or possibly before, the weavers had evolved into the beginnings of a co-operative movement of the people, the first to be formalised anywhere in the world. There were co-operative cornmills in Chatham and Woolwich in 1760 and the idea of co-operation wasn't new then, but Fenwick was the first we would recognise as a co-op. They started with oatmeal, the Scottish staple, buying sacks of it wholesale and selling it to society members at a good discount. They did this using the cottage of a founder member, John Walker, as their shop. They also bought books, which led to the Fenwick Library, 1808. Any money left over as profit was distributed back to the members, but money was also lent at a flat rate of interest, and some was given to those in severe need.

The decline in hand weaving and the rise in Scottish emigration, helped in no small measure by the society's own policy of assisting people in moving abroad, reduced the population of the village so much that the society withered away and died in 1873. By then it had been imitated in Greenock, Glasgow, Oldham and elsewhere

There were twenty-eight original members of the Rochdale Equitable Pioneers Society. Thirteen of them in this picture are: (back row, left to right) James Manock (flannel weaver), John Collier (engineer), Samuel Ashworth, William Cooper (flannel weavers), James Tweedale (clogger), Joseph Smith (woolsorter); (front row, left to right) James Standring (flannel weaver), John Bent (tailor), James Smithies (woolsorter), Charles Howarth (warper), David Brooks (block printer), Benjamin Rudman (flannel weaver), John Scowcroft (hawker).

and, consciously or unconsciously, by a much more famous co-op, the one founded by the Rochdale Pioneers in 1844.

There were twenty-eight pioneers, all local to Rochdale, all with left-wing views and a high-minded, rebellious spirit. They were relatively well off, being skilled workers or self-employed tradesmen, but their ideals brought them together on behalf of all working people, especially the poorer ones who were being defrauded of what little they had by the company store system. You worked in the mill, got your wages, and spent them on bad quality, adulterated goods in the shop run by the mill owner.

The Pioneers' new shop was in Toad Lane, Rochdale, on the street where, eleven years earlier, a Rochdale Friendly Society had tried to start a co-op. This was the thing with co-ops. They started all over the place, especially in the Manchester area, but always fizzled out due to lack of expertise and determination.

The Rochdale Pioneers would be different. They sold only the basics at first; flour, butter, candles, tea and oatmeal, two nights a week. Samuel Ashworth (see murky picture, third from left, back row) was the sales assistant, and he handed the takings over to William Cooper (standing on Ashworth's left), cashier. After only three months' trading they were open four nights a week, had a wider range of goods for sale, and at the end of their first year had seventy-four members. That rose to 400 members in 1849, the year that the Rochdale Savings Bank collapsed after its director, mill owner George Howarth, embezzled the money and proved to the workers of Rochdale that it was the rich what got the pleasure and the poor what got the blame. The remedy had to be in their own hands, in the form of co-operation.

So successful were they that delegations came from around the world to see how a co-op could actually work and stay in business. Co-operative societies sprang up all over again, and co-operated, forming the Co-operative Manufacturing Society in 1863, the first venture being a biscuit factory, which became the CWS, the Wholesale Society, in 1872, based at No. 1 Balloon Street, Manchester, an address that was to feature on untold millions of marmalade jars, tins of peas, tins of peaches, packets of tea and bottles of sauce.

Before very long, there was hardly a community without its own co-operative society, buying its goods from the CWS. Your correspondent in particular remembers the Brandon and Byshottles Co-operative Society, serving the mining village of Brandon, County Durham, and surrounding district. This was universally referred to as 'The Store', and branches of it, with associated activities such as

insurance and funeral direction, served every need from cradle to grave. People put green tokens on their doorsteps with their empty bottles for the Co-op milkman to exchange. Loyalty to The Store never wavered, not even when the *News of the World* ran its famous

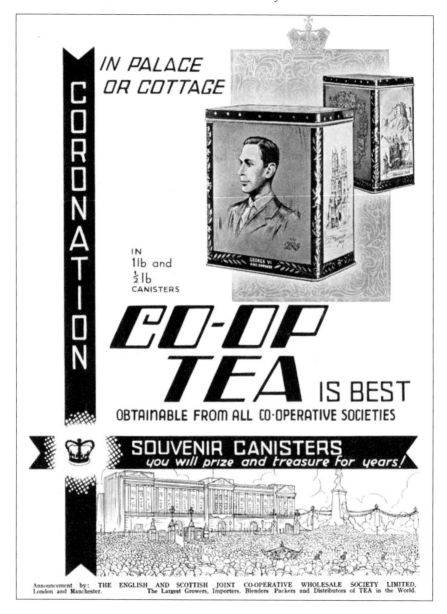

headline: 'Woman elopes with Chinese foreman of Co-op bacon factory'.

In modern times, as the supermarket chains began to spread, the old Co-op struggled. Being a democratic organisation and run by

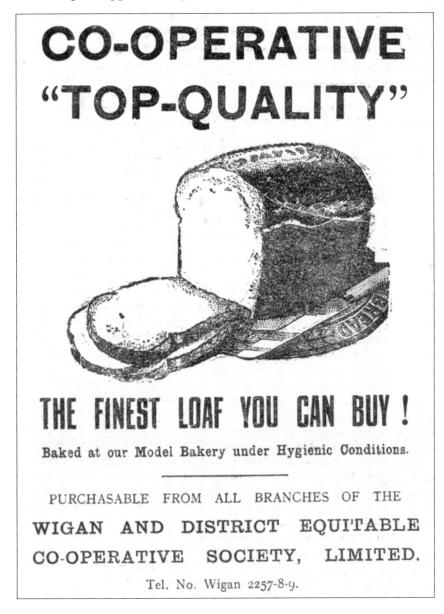

CO-OPERATIVE "TOP-QUALITY"

THE FINEST LOAF YOU CAN BUY !

Baked at our Model Bakery under Hygienic Conditions.

PURCHASABLE FROM ALL BRANCHES OF THE

WIGAN AND DISTRICT EQUITABLE CO-OPERATIVE SOCIETY, LIMITED.

Tel. No. Wigan 2257-8-9.

a very large committee, the CWS was unable to respond speedily or decisively. It harked back to its noble principles while more aggressive grocers stole its business. The Co-op as a whole also had the unique handicap of being hundreds of small, independent societies, each also run by committee, and therefore having to close numbers of its own shops and terminate its own members wherever it opened a new supermarket.

Its sheer size and the massive spread of its activities helped it survive. It was, and is, Britain's biggest farmer, biggest funeral director, big optician, big travel agent, dominant milk supplier in many parts, insurer of one in six families, bankers to many also. It's full of strange statistics, like it makes 10 per cent of all the UK's glass jars and bottles, blends 16,000 tonnes of tea a year, won first, second and third prizes in a *Which?* whisky test with its own-label Scotch. It has dozens of stores where no other large company would – Tobermory, Isle of Mull, for instance – and all with that extra ethical, caring dimension.

Slowly the Co-op has hauled itself into the brave new world of shopping, with Fair Trade and a somewhat less voracious image than certain of its competitors. Inevitably, the side effect has been to shut down in many, many high streets where it had once been on every one.

Thomas Wall

Wall's never had any shops but we shall make an exception in recounting such a curious tale of royal sausages, a donkey, fish, some tricycles, and a considerable number of Thomas Walls. The first one we know about was born in 1817 in St James's, Westminster, son of Richard Wall who had been apprenticed to a pork butcher called Cotterill whose shop was only a few doors away from the home of the Prince of Wales who was later to become George IV.

It ain't what you know, it's who you know, and Cotterill supplied pork, in sausages and otherwise, to the prince's household at Carlton House and, when Richard Wall took over the business, this excellent trade continued. Indeed, the Prince Regent, which George had become owing to the madness of his father, granted Wall a Royal Warrant. This he renewed when he became king, and his younger brother did the same when he came to the throne as William IV.

Four years into his latest warrant, Richard, the first sausage king, removed to finer premises in Jermyn Street and there moved up a gear as regards technology. He installed some industrial-quality mincing and mixing machinery in the cellar, and bought a well-behaved donkey to walk around and around, driving the machine. It is not known what the health and safety inspectors of the age thought about donkeys and sausage meat in such close proximity, or if the king ever found a donkey hair in his breakfast, but the method certainly worked well for Wall.

He died in 1838 and his widow ran the show while her son, our first Thomas, made himself acquainted with the trade and, presumably, the arts and crafts of donkey management. This Thomas married well, to a Mary Charlton, daughter of a man who didn't work, i.e. a gentleman, and shortly found himself also warranted by Queen Victoria. Thomas and Mary's first son was born in 1846 and they called him Thomas. He was apprenticed to his papa as soon as he was old enough and taken into the partnership, as was his brother Fred, and thus the firm became Thomas Wall and Sons in 1878.

The Wall brothers concentrated entirely on high quality products for the upper end of the market, supplying the best hotels, the best restaurants, the leading department stores and the wealthiest private households. They didn't advertise; they didn't need to. Thomas was the administrator, the chairman, while Frederick oversaw production, of sausages, pies and various other porky things.

Production in fact became their biggest problem. Their success increased demand but they never could seem to sort out a factory. They had three small facilities in different places. Despite rising costs from this inefficiency and from ingredients getting more and more expensive, Thomas refused at first to raise his prices. The firm, now T Wall and Sons Ltd, made a loss for the first time, in several of the years leading up to the First World War.

The other big problem was Thomas himself. He was hardly ever there. By far his main interest in life was not in making money but giving it away. He supported pretty well any charity that asked, particularly if it was an educational one and/or linked to young people. He founded the Thomas Wall Trust, which is still going and still giving grants to struggling students. He gave money for playing fields, he gave it to the YMCA, the WEA, the scouts, and assumed the sausages would keep on supporting his benevolence without any interference from him.

Brother Fred was doing his job, as was everyone else, but there was no direction:

> *'Thomas, what should we do about the annual sales slump in the summer?'*
>   *'No idea.'*
>   *'Where are you going now?'*
>   *'Church, then a meeting of the Adult School Movement.'*

Circling around, waiting to pounce, was the perfect predator, a man who could spot a business opportunity from any distance, a man who could see what was needed at Wall's. William Hesketh Lever, founder of Lever Brothers, bought the company, moved meat production to one large factory and solved the summer slackness by pushing the firm into ice cream.

Very few shops in those days had freezers, so the ice cream had to be sold another way. The answer was the famous tricycle with metal-lined wooden cool box up front, ridden by a fellow in a uniform and cap that made him look like an RAC patrolman. This fellow must have been strong in the legs because those trikes were hard work to propel when empty, never mind when full of ice cream, and how grateful he must have been when someone took notice of the slogan painted on his box, and stopped him and bought one.

Lever also provided a new sales outlet for the sausages: MacFisheries. He rightly thought that such a product would sit well with his fresh fish, and Wall's went from strength to strength. Lever Brothers cuddled up to the Dutch margarine industry and became Unilever in 1929 and Thomas, who had insisted on the ice-cream trike-riders going to church first if they were riding out on a Sunday, died in 1930. The trikes were requisitioned for the war effort and, in 1947, Wall's sold over 3,000 of them and bought freezers for shops instead.

Wall's ice cream is still part of Unilever but the sausages, along with Porkinson's and Bowyer's, belong to the Ireland-based Kerry

Group, which delivers 'technology-based integrated solutions to the food industry', it says here. Possibly that wouldn't involve a donkey, not even Delaney's donkey.

Your correspondent was taking a tour around a sausage factory some years ago – the firm shall remain nameless, except to say it wasn't Wall's – and they were making four qualities of banger. Top quality was Marks & Spencer own label, second was their own brand, third was catering quality, and last was 'prisons and mental homes'.

William Whiteley

Born in 1831, the son of a West Riding corn merchant, William Whiteley led a remarkable life, even by high street hero standards, and ended in a truly sensational death. He started quietly enough, leaving school at 14 as so many did, and working on his uncle's farm for a couple of years until being accepted as a draper's apprentice by Harnew & Glover in Northgate, Wakefield.

He was 20 when he took a train to London to see the Great Exhibition of 1851 in the Crystal Palace. Somehow, elements of that experience reacted with his ambition to make a mark on the world, and the compound result was the Whiteley notion of another, quite different kind of palace: a shopping one.

He was a careful Yorkshire lad, this William, and he planned his route to fame with care and precision. First, he would move permanently to London and set about acquiring the broad understanding of the trade he felt he needed, over and above his knowledge of drapery in Wakefield. He would work for a London draper (Willey's in Ludgate), a wholesaler (the Fore Street Warehouse) and a haberdasher (probably a firm called Leat & Sons), save all his pennies, and then make the leap.

It took him eight years, living on almost nothing, never going out and never spending any money beyond what was absolutely necessary for subsistence, until he felt he had enough – £700 – to found his business. This was a substantial sum of money in 1863, something like £250,000 if you take an average of the various historical financial indices, and we can only wonder at the dedication of a young man who could save that kind of amount from ordinary clerical and junior-management wages. A manual worker at that time might earn half-a-crown a day, which is fifteen shillings for a six-day week. A smart chap in a good retailing job could earn twice that, maybe more, but even if we guess that William Whiteley was earning £2 10s a week, and was doing no other deals on the side, he would have had to save two-thirds of his income.

So, he had his capital, but where would he go? The more obvious places like Oxford Street didn't appeal financially, so he chose Bayswater, originally a hamlet in the parish of Paddington known for its freshwater springs. By this time Bayswater, according to a contemporary description, 'formed a large suburban town', a mile west of Marble Arch, in the county of Middlesex, borough of Marylebone. Whiteley believed this unremarkable suburb was on the up.

He saw the premises he wanted in Westbourne Grove, bought in stocks of fancy goods, ribbons, buttons and bows, and hired two young ladies as assistants. To one he took a particular shine, Miss Hill, Hattie to her friends, and they married after a longish courtship in 1867.

That was four years after opening, twelve years after moving to London with nothing, or almost nothing. It is said he had £10 in his pocket, let's say about £3,500 in today's money. In that time, not only had he talked Hattie Hill into marriage, but he'd extended his little haberdashery shop into seventeen different departments, and a few years on it was almost a street of shops, eighteen in a row. This expansion was not always fully appreciated by local residents who found their outlook blighted by more and more buildings as Whiteley moved into Queen's Road.

Like Smith, Burton and Woolworth, Whiteley was another who saw the value of a corporate identity, an immediately recognisable trademark, and his idea was *Universal Provider*, the phrase put beside a representation of the world in two hemispheres. He would supply everything to everyone, from *an immense symposium of the arts and industries of the nation and of the world*. When someone tested him by ordering an elephant, he got hold of one the same day. Now, he could claim to be able to supply *everything from a pin to an elephant*.

He did add some quite unusual services for a department store, including an estate agency and a building and decorating division, but he kept on growing, under royal patronage too. By 1890 he employed 6,000 people, and that despite a number of fires, almost certainly arson attacks by local competitors, smaller shopkeepers who felt they were being overwhelmed by a gargantuan (so you see, there's nothing new under the sun). William was convinced he was being deliberately targeted by fire-raisers, so he hired his own permanent firemen, installed steel firebreak doors between departments, and instructed that hoses should be connected to stand-pipes every evening as the shop closed, so they could be instantly ready.

These measures were of little help in 1885 when the three buildings, each of five floors which housed the millinery and linens departments, were entirely destroyed and three other buildings badly damaged. It might have been even worse without the experience of the previous three fires, so that London's noble Fire Brigade, by the ringing of alarm bells and judicious use of the new telephone, could summon the immediate aid of thirteen steam-powered fire engines, plus five more from outlying districts. Whiteley's stock was uninsured, as no insurer was willing to take the risk, and the buildings were only partly covered.

The greatest of the fires occurred in 1887. Indeed, it was the greatest fire seen in London in that century. Three men were killed by falling masonry and a fire engine was completely buried without fatalities. One of the dead, on removal to Paddington Baths, was identified as Whiteley's night watchman, Albert Blake, which misfortune his wife and son were invited to confirm. Mrs Blake was certain it was her husband. The son said it couldn't be, because the body wore a collar and his father had never worn such a thing in his life. The argument continued until Mr Blake himself walked into the room.

After so many fires, Whiteley could hardly get any insurance at all and had to replenish and rebuild from his own pocket. Business must have been very good, and it had to be as usual. He wrote to the papers:

Sir, – May I beg the favour of your making the announcement in the columns of The Times *that, notwithstanding the fire that took place at my Queen's Road premises on Saturday last is the most calamitous that has yet occurred, I have been enabled to complete arrangements for carrying on the business of every department without delay or inconvenience to my customers?*

Good old William. He was the man who could watch squillions go up in smoke, and then complete arrangements for carrying on.

There was another side to Whiteley, a strict and authoritarian employer of those 6,000, issuing dozens and scores of petty rules that had to be kept, under penalty of fines or dismissal. Many of the staff lived in company dormitories, although 'lived' is rather overstating it as many of them worked sixteen-hour days with only Sundays off.

This attitude to other people was in some contrast to Whiteley's set of rules for his own behaviour, which allowed him frequent trips to Hove in the late 1870s with his friend, a stockbroker called George Rayner. William probably thought he deserved a bit of fun after all those years of austerity when he was saving up for his first shop, and the fun in this case was provided by two sisters, Louisa and Emily Turner.

It seems that some mistress-swapping went on, because when Emily had a baby boy, although he went to live with Rayner and took that name, in later years this Horace Rayner was told his real father was William Whiteley. Meanwhile, William separated from Hattie – they had four children – and set Louisa up in a London house, where she had a son. *The Times* of 2 August 1882 reported that Mrs Harriet Sarah Whiteley had petitioned the Court for the dissolution of her marriage on the grounds of adultery and cruelty, but they settled for living apart with Hattie on an annual allowance of £2,000.

A few years after the last rebuild of 1887, the store passed the magic mark of £1 million in turnover (let's say £250 million in our terms) and was floated as a public company. Whiteley stepped back from the business, leaving the running to his two sons, William junior and Frank, but still turned up every day, in top hat and frock coat, to conduct his round of inspection.

On the 24th of January 1907, he was doing just that when a man in his late 20s came up to him, a fellow the 75-year-old William knew well, and who brought back happy memories of dalliances in Hove. Horace Rayner, also known as Horace Turner, was unemployed, stony broke, and he wanted a job from the man he claimed as his father. He'd had an up-and-down career, including a spell as a sales rep in Russia, and he was married with two children. He didn't mention in this interview that he was also engaged to a barmaid, who knew him as Horace Payne. After half an hour, Whiteley would still have none of it, even though Horace had pulled a gun and put it to his own head in despair. The old man was treating the approach as blackmail and, coming out onto the shop floor, he asked an assistant to go for a policeman. Horace emerged and William was seen, waving the young man away. 'Are you going to give in?' said Horace. 'No,' said William, and that was that. Horace shot him dead, with two bullets to the head.

Horace then tried to shoot himself, succeeded but not fatally, and recovered to face trial for murder, during which a suicide note was read out showing that Horace had indeed intended to kill William and himself. Horace's wife said he was prone to depression, apparently carrying the burden of a great secret. Much evidence was produced to show that William could not have been the father of his killer, including a witness statement from Louisa Turner, and much to show that Rayner was not the father either. It appeared that Emily Turner had had two sons, both by Rayner, or not, and one was possibly Louisa's anyway. The frivolities in Hove were not mentioned.

The jury took ten minutes to find Horace guilty. The judge automatically sentenced him to death, saying there was not the slightest hope of the sentence not being carried out. However, it was commuted. A petition was got up by Rayner's solicitor, attracting 179,000 signatures, and the Home Secretary swiftly intervened – so swiftly, in fact, that he acted before the petition had been presented.

'In view of all the circumstances, (the Home Secretary) had felt warranted in advising His Majesty to respite the capital sentence, with a view to its commutation to penal servitude for life.' In view of what circumstances, we ask? In those days, going up to someone with a gun and shooting him dead could hardly result in anything other than a hanging.

The Home Secretary in question, Herbert Gladstone, eldest son of the famous Prime Minister William Ewart Gladstone, was not widely known for his intellectual capacity or his ability to keep his nerve under pressure. Later, Asquith would fire him and send him off to be Governor of South Africa, which was one way of dealing with thick toffs in the olden days.

147

A writer to *The Times*, a barrister and ex-MP, suggested that a retrial by public opinion was being substituted for trial by jury according to law, and demanded 'a clear and authoritative explanation of this apparently hasty and mysterious reprieve, for which no official reason has been given. Otherwise, direct encouragement will be afforded to all potential blackmailers and homicides, and the habitual carrying of a revolver for self-defence will become a commercial and social necessity.' No explanation ever was given, and Rayner, killer of our only high street hero to suffer a violent death, was released in 1919.

Frank Winfield Woolworth

> *There's a famous seaside place called Blackpool,*
> *That's noted for fresh air and fun,*
> *And Mr. and Mrs. Ramsbottom*
> *Went there with young Albert, their son.*
>
> *A grand little lad was young Albert,*
> *All dressed in his best; quite a swell*
> *With a stick with an 'orse's 'ead 'andle,*
> *The finest that Woolworth's could sell.*

For those that don't know the story of *Albert and the Lion* by Marriot Edgar, the stick in question proves to be Albert's nemesis. Seeking to enliven a sleepy lion by shoving his Woolworth's stick in its ear, he only succeeds in becoming the lion's dinner. For those that do know Woolworth's, which must be just about everybody, the meaning of 'The finest that Woolworth's could sell' will be quite clear. This horse-headed stick was a cheap treat for a little boy of a certain class, who was used to modest standards. That was the image of Woolies, and it was quite deliberate. From his earliest times in business, Frank Woolworth was after a little money from a lot of people who didn't have much.

Son of John Hubbell Woolworth of Pinckney and Fanny McBrier of Brownville, he was born in 1852, on a farm near the township of Rodman in Jefferson County, New York. The family moved to Champion, in that county, in 1859. Frank went to the village school, and then to business college in Watertown, an education that was not as grand as it sounds. In the USA at that time, there was a shortage of young men of clerical bent and it was commonplace for someone to set up a private school where book-keeping, penmanship and other business basics could be taught.

From there, F W went to work for a Mr Bushnell, who had a shop in Watertown, but left when Bushnell refused him a rise in wages. He moved down the street to Moore and Smith's dry goods store. It is said that Frank Woolworth had a bright idea while working at Moore and Smith's. Instead of keeping all that miscellaneous inventory from year to year, all those little items that never did sell and probably never would, we should offer them at a really cheap price. At least we'll get something for them, and such a sale could bring customers in who then might buy more expensive things. Well, that's one version of the story.

It is also said that having a clearance sale was a regular thing for Moore and Smith, with everything at five cents, and young Frank saw this and was deeply impressed.

However the idea might have come about, Master Woolworth got the loan of a few barrowloads of junk from his employers and set up a stall of his own in Utaca, in 1879. It failed because, F W believed, his choice of location had been poor. So he set up again, in a fairly down-at-heel district of Lancaster, Pennsylvania in 1881, and there he added ten-cent items to his five-cent range. This time, he had it just right. Woolworth's went off like a rocket.

He expanded partly by using his own profits and partly by creating partnerships with men whom he then installed as managers. As the key to success with customers was price, the key for F W had to be great variety of goods bought in as economically as possible. By the time he decided to start selling sweets, he had enough clout to be able to bypass wholesalers and purchase in bulk direct from the manufacturers.

Another factor was recognition by people on the street. Like the cowboy with his branding iron, Woolworth needed to impress his mark in a way that could not be rubbed out. Like Burton and W H Smith over in Britain, he saw the benefit of a company identity. He insisted on a unified style of window display, devised by himself, and came up with the famous red design to mark all his shop fronts, the numbers of which were increasing at a phenomenal rate. In the twenty years from 1890, Woolworth opened 600 stores. That included his first in the UK, in Liverpool, and he went on to open forty more British stores by the outbreak of the First World War. Instead of the American five and ten cents, the sterling equivalent was threepence and sixpence.

In 1912, Woolworth merged with some of his leading competitors and the next year opened the Woolworth Building in New York, then the tallest in the world. His triumphs were not to glitter for long. His eldest daughter Edna had made a bad marriage with a wealthy but philandering and alcoholic banker. She had an affair with the man who would one day be the father of Jackie Kennedy / Onassis, and F W urged divorce. Unable to cope, Edna committed suicide, her body being discovered by her own child, Frank's granddaughter, the 6-year-old Barbara Hutton, another sad case who would inherit a huge fortune and go through seven husbands, mostly glamorous European aristocrats but including one film star, Cary Grant.

F W never would go to the dentist. As a result of his fear of the drill and the pliers, he contracted a severe infection in his mouth in 1919, in the age long before antibiotics, and there was nothing to be done to save him. He died a multi-multi-millionaire with over 1,000 five-and-dimes and threepence and tanners. The 400th UK shop opened in Southport, 1930, and the 800th in London Victoria in 1953. At the peak, there were almost 1,150 branches in Britain.

By 1970, there were 4,000 Woolies altogether but the retailing style hadn't evolved with the times. Cracks were appearing as competitors carved off pieces of the trade. The American parent sold its British offspring in 1982 and the newly independent business tried a thousand ploys to stay alive. In the US, the firm was reborn as Venator in 1997, then again as its most successful division, Foot Locker, in which guise it continues to thrive, selling trainers in over 1,000 outlets.

In the UK, back down to 800 shops, Woolworth's went into administration with debts of around £400 million, and all branches were closed after Christmas 2008. The name joined Shop Direct, alongside Littlewood's, Kay's and Great Universal Stores, and carries on as web pages. Some of the shop sites have been bought by other chains, and some have been relaunched on similar lines to the original.

Old Wooliesians will remember Embassy Records at 78 rpm, those cheap covers of hit songs, remade by session musicians and club singers. Then there was Winfield, the Woolies equivalent of St Michael and the founder's middle name, of course. Ladybird children's clothes were made by various companies, latterly Coats Viyella, but sold only by Woolworth which bought the name in 2001, and it's still there on the aforesaid web pages, selling very well.

As we write, it's 120 years since F W Woolworth, bruised by his experience in Utaca, was looking for a better place to start his dream. How are the mighty fallen.

CHAPTER 4

Where did it all go wrong?

We went to those high street shops to buy things. So what happened to so many of the things we used to buy? Whatever happened to Eiffel Tower Puddings, Flit and the Flit gun, Parkinson's Biscuits, and Lavvo, for spotless lavatories? You can't get Medilax laxative pellets, with the good effect that lasted several days. Benger's Food, which used to require very little effort on the part of the digestive organs, now requires no effort at all.

Cremona Toffee gained a knighthood for its inventor, Albert Wilkin, but was bought by Rowntree Mackintosh and disappeared. Pumphrey's Lemon Curd, once a delicacy at any time, is a delicacy no more. Camp coffee is still available in Scotland and Canada at least, while Mackintosh's Toffee-de-Luxe, delicious beyond description, has no description now.

Eno's Fruit Salt, it's a pleasure to drink, still sells lots in foreign markets although not in the UK, and Twilfit corsets, British-made throughout, are now Swedish. Spry, the ready-creamed fat, was produced by Unilever from 1936 until the 1960s, when regiments of women stopped baking cakes.

Mansion Polish, a bright and healthy home in every tin, could be had in rose perfume or antiseptic. Phillips Stick-a-Soles never would stick for long, unlike Tattoo Lipstick – put it on, let it set, wipe it off. It's divine. It's distinctive. Or there was Tangee Lipstick in six shades of loveliness, including Gay Red and Pink Queen.

Mrs Peek's Puddings came in tins – Xmas, Light Fruit, Dark Fruit, Date, Ginger and Sultana – and with too much of that with your supper, you might have a terrible dream. You might dream you went to work in your Maidenform bra (and you still can).

Remember Spangles? Square with rounded corners and circular dips on either side, fruit-flavoured. Once you'd managed to open the pack in the darkness of the cinema, you found a sticky sweet impossible to unwrap and you ended up putting it in your mouth with some of the Cellophane still on. Later, they used waxed paper, and various other sorts came out like Old English Spangles. Invented by Mars around 1950 during sweet rationing, Spangles were discontinued in the early 1980s apart from a short-lived rally at Woolies.

Whatever happened to Bile Beans? Here is the text from an advertisement published in 1932:

WHO ARE THE GIRLS WHO MARRY?

Wake Up, You Girls,

and Realise the Priceless Secret Of Happy Matrimony.

Beauty alone will lure few men to the altar. The sterner sex is interested in the physically-fit woman rather than the pretty-pretty girl.

Nice features must always be accompanied by vivaciousness, vitality, and personality. The greatest of these is the vitality born of rich red blood coursing through the veins, which is the real giver of the bloom of youth. By taking Bile Beans at bedtime you can acquire a clear, soft complexion, sweet breath, and sparkling health.

The Bile Bean girl is the girl who is clean and healthy inside, and with her vivacity she has the world at her feet. She's the girl who has the looks and the sweet temper with which to win and keep the best husband.

Send for a free sample of BILE BEANS.

Bile Beans, the ventriloquist's nightmare, were a quite complex patent medicine invented in Australia in 1899, being a mixture of laxatives, things to expel wind and things to shift bile. Bile, or gall, that horrible greeny-black-yellowish substance secreted into the

154

digestive process can, if faced with excesses on the food and drink front, react rebelliously to produce bilious attacks.

The marketing aimed straight at women. The promises were for women. Bile Beans were supposed to make peace in the duodenum and, by assuring the same kind of inner cleanliness as Andrew's Liver Salts, render the person taking them several invaluable services, such as slimness, brightness of the eye and that most elusive quality of all, the ability to win and keep the best husband.

Bile Beans disappeared from the market as trade descriptions began to bite hard, people realised that laxatives were largely unnecessary, and the definition of 'best husband' became the subject of debate.

While various manufacturers tried to persuade us to be clean on the inside, there was also the outside to think about:

ICILMA – the Anti-Grease Cream

Entirely free from grease, yet without the slightest drying action on the skin, Icilma forms a perfect base for powder and is guaranteed not to grow hair. Unique in containing the famous beautifying Icilma water from Algeria, it protects and does good to the skin.

ICILMA

THE CREAM OF SOCIETY

That was in 1926, when the main thrust of Icilma promotion was to the upper end of the market: I told Lady Sarah how to look good on a horse, that sort of thing. By the late 1940s, magazines such as *Good Housekeeping* and *Vogue* were running ads featuring a girl caught in an embarrassing moment by 'him', such as ironing her undies or letting the milk boil over, and being thankful that she'd applied her Icilma cream and powder. Unexpected encounters will never worry you. You'll always be sure your complexion is smooth and matt. And we guarantee you won't be growing hair.

Not in my shop window. In olden days a glimpse of stocking was looked on as something shocking, and the shock might have been all the more eye-widening had the glimpse been of Ballito pure

Volumes of Good Wishes

This is the happiest way . . . the most unusual way to send that most acceptable present on your Christmas list. Two or three pairs of **ballito** stockings in this "Novel" pack (see the list of prices below). In **ballito** you have the finest value your shillings can buy.

BEAUTIFUL

ballito *pure silk* **stockings**

Made at the **ballito** all-British modern Factories at St. Albans

ballito *Pure Silk*

STOCKINGS

ballito 2/- stockings . . . . . 3 pairs in box 5/11   **ballito** 2/11½ stockings . . 2 pairs in box 5/11
ballito 3/11½ stockings . . 2 pairs in box 7/11   **ballito** 4/11 stockings . . . 2 pairs in box 9/9
ballito 6/11 stockings . . 2 pairs in box 13/9

silk, made in St Albans. At two shillings a pair (standard quality) in 1936, up to 6s 11d a pair for the very finest, such luxury was not everyone's. Taking into account average wages, that 6/11 would be about £65 in modern money. Two pairs at 13/9 saved one of those heavy old pennies, and you got a Christmas box made to look like a book.

Ballito became part of Courtaulds, since when the name has disappeared from everywhere except the vintage clothing section of eBay. The factory is now a supermarket.

Barker & Dobson, Callard & Bowser, Clarnico, Needler's, Carson's Dorchester chocolates – what names to conjure with. Barker & Dobson began in early Victorian times but didn't really get moving until the turn of that century, under the stewardship of the third generation, Percy and Henry Jacobson. They are credited with the idea of wrapping sweets individually, which means they are to blame for a lot of sticky fingers.

B&D had become a huge firm by the start of the Second World War, making over 400 different sorts of sweets including, obviously, Cameo chocolates and Regal fruit drops and, probably best known, Everton mints.

In 1986, Barker & Dobson bought Budgens supermarkets for an 'audacious' £80 million. In 1988, after trying and failing to take over Dee Supermarkets, they decided to be Budgens only, so sold their confectionery operations and the B&D name to a Scottish outfit called Alma Caledonian (Keiller's Dundee marmalade). From there, B&D went to Trebor Bassett, who formed a company called Monkhill Confectionery that included B&D brands, and that was part of Cadbury Schweppes for a while but was taken over in 2008 by a new company, Tangerine, whose brands now include Lion, Pascall, Butterkist, Sharp's Toffees which is called Taveners, and more, and a small range of Barker & Dobson.

Callard & Bowser, incidentally, found its way into the Kraft organisation but ended up with Suchard. Remember Callard & Bowser butterscotch, and the nougat with cherries and nuts wrapped in rice paper, and Creamline and liquorice toffees? Well, remember away, because Suchard have stopped making any C&B lines.

157

Is it a bird? Is it a car? Lawrie Bond, 1907–1974, was primarily interested in racing cars and he designed several, including the 500cc Bond Special which was about the size of a child's pedal car. Another commercial interest for the Bond Aircraft and Engineering

SUPREME in its CLASS
THE Bond MINICAR

- **85** M.P.G.
- **50** M.P.H.
- **£5** TAX

1958

FROM
£279
Family Models for
2 adults and
2 children

THE WORLD'S BEST
THREE WHEELER!

Hardtop
convertible coupe
2 to 3 seater

·Backed by 300 distributors, dealers and
service agents throughout the British Isles.

BOND MINICAR WORKS · PRESTON · LANCS

Company was small motorbikes and scooters. None of this was very successful but Lawrie hit the spot in 1948 with his idea for a 'shopping car', the Bond Minicar, 'the most economical car in the world'. With a light aluminium body and a 122cc Villiers motor-cycle engine, it could do 40 mph and over 100 miles to the gallon. You could certainly go to the shops cheaply in it but you couldn't buy much unless you went on your own because, with two people aboard, the sole destination for shopping had to be a basket on the passenger's knee. The only part of the car with lots of room was under the bonnet, where a seemingly vast and airy space had a tiny engine in the middle that looked like it ought to be powering a model aeroplane.

Slightly more sophisticated models of the Bond Minicar came later. The ones in the ad (cheer up, madam, you're going shopping, not to your own funeral) are the Mark F (top) and Mark D. In fifteen years, well over 25,000 Bond Minicars were made in Preston by a firm called Sharp's Commercials.

The last model, the Mark G, had a 246cc Villiers engine and its features included doors, which earlier models had lacked, four seats, suspension at the rear and wind-up windows. Alas for the G, its introduction at the 1959 motor show was somewhat overshadowed by another debutant, the Austin Mini Minor. The finger of doom was pointing and, with competition hotting up from the Reliant Regal, by 1966 they thought it was all over. And it was.

Chocolate to march on. Albert Caley was a mineral-waters maker who went in for chocolate in Norwich in 1883; the company was highly successful, also making Christmas crackers. There was a large factory for Mackintosh's to take over in 1932, and for the Germans to destroy with their bombs in 1942. It was reopened in 1947, bought out by Rowntree and so to Nestlé, closed in 1996 and demolished to make way for the Chapelfield shopping centre.

Your correspondent remembers the scent of chocolate drifting in the Norwich air in the late 1970s and, longer ago, a sixpenny bar of his youth called Caley Tray, which was six milk chocolates of the sort you had in a box but sitting together, joined by chocolate,

Melting coffee creams and truffles, marzipan and crispy nuts . . . . . . eleven delicious centres and you don't know where to begin ? Then shut your eyes, twiddle a finger, *pounce!*

CALEY *make wonderful chocolates*

A. J. CALEY LIMITED, NORWICH

ready to be snapped off one at a time and possibly including a hazelnut whirl.

Some executives of the old firm bought the brand from Nestlé, and the company has been reborn as Caley's of Norwich, based in Hampshire, offering nostalgic products harking back to the First World War such as Marching Chocolate, in Fair Trade modern versions, and drinking chocolate in their cafe not far from where the factory used to be.

What you won't find at a tobacconist, if you could find a tobacconist. You just don't get amazing advertising offers like you used to. This one (on next page), from 1928, gives you a free bottle of perfume with every shilling box of Turkish cigarettes, some of which are tipped with a rose petal, some with silk, some with gold, and all of the rarest vintage that could grace the banquet of thoughts. Normally only available in the harems of Constantinople or the palaces of India's Native Princes, these smokes are scented with an extract of amber, usually priced at a guinea an ounce but free at your tobacconist (or harem or palace, if that's easier). A guinea an ounce, for younger readers would translate today as £200 for 25 grams.

161

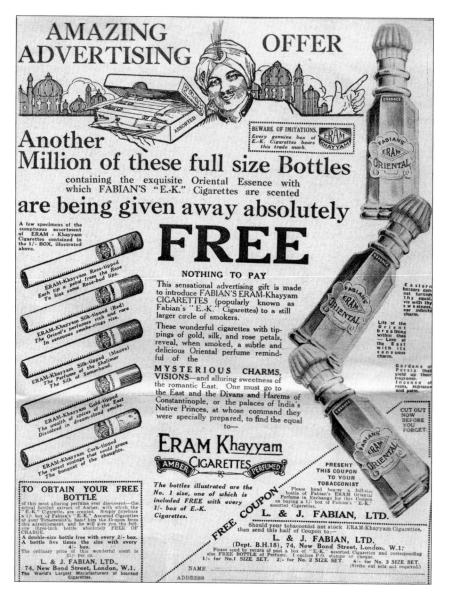

Cars in the High Street. A Ford Zephyr 6 is here adjudged to be sufficiently amphibious by its driver to attempt Weymouth high street in August 1955, after 7 inches (18 cm) of rain had fallen in twenty-one hours. Some cars parked on lower ground were completely submerged as the water overwhelmed all defences.

The greatest loss in advertising seems to be in the lack of faith of the public in the advertising. If people gave more credence to advertising, much less of it would be needed to secure the same result.

P H Nystrom,
Elements of Retail Selling, 1936.

A very good point this is, Mr Nystrom, and the reason is a simple one. When there were no restraints on advertising, people told lies. When better standards were demanded, people found other, more sophisticated ways of persuading us to buy, without stating simple facts such as 'No matter how much Eastern Foam Vanishing Cream you clart on your face, you'll never get rid of that wart and your freckles will never vanish'.

The ad for Nescafé on page 165 begins by knocking its own best claim to fame: the coffee is instant, a new thing in the early 1950s. The first ads for the first instant coffee, Nescafé, naturally emphasised its Unique Selling Proposition, but sales were disappointing. This

163

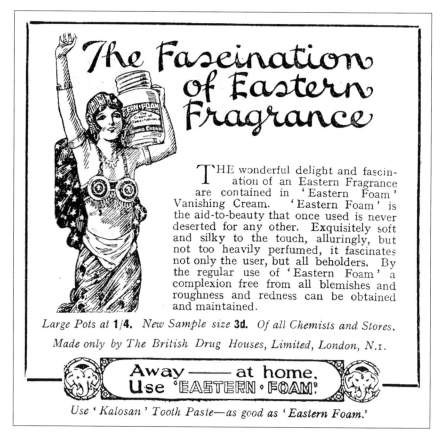

The Fascination of Eastern Fragrance

THE wonderful delight and fascination of an Eastern Fragrance are contained in 'Eastern Foam' Vanishing Cream. 'Eastern Foam' is the aid-to-beauty that once used is never deserted for any other. Exquisitely soft and silky to the touch, alluringly, but not too heavily perfumed, it fascinates not only the user, but all beholders. By the regular use of 'Eastern Foam' a complexion free from all blemishes and roughness and redness can be obtained and maintained.

Large Pots at **1/4**. *New Sample size* **3d**. *Of all Chemists and Stores.*

Made only by The British Drug Houses, Limited, London, N.1.

Away —— at home. Use 'EASTERN·FOAM.'

Use 'Kalosan' Tooth Paste—as good as 'Eastern Foam.'

was in America; our idea of instant coffee in Britain at the time was Camp.

A survey was made by the ad agency, using two grocery shopping lists which were identical except for the coffee. One list had a pound bag of Maxwell House, then exclusively a brand of ground coffee, and one had a packet of Nescafé. The people surveyed were asked to draw inferences from the list about the character of the housewife doing the shopping.

Those shown the list with Maxwell House said this shopper was obviously a good wife and mother who cared about feeding her family properly. Those shown the list with Nescafé basically said she was a lazy bitch. Hence, in the ads, they began downplaying the instant-ness and played up the coffee-ness. Nescafé never looked back.

there's always time for Nescafé

If you're somewhat conservative about coffee-making, the quickness and simplicity of Nescafé may not be its strongest claim with you. But — put a teaspoonful of Nescafé in a cup, add piping hot water, milk and sugar to taste, and see if you don't agree that Nescafé makes *good* coffee — enjoyable from the first waft of roaster-fresh fragrance to the last full-flavoured drop.

NESCAFÉ

for grand coffee quickly

Nescafé is a soluble coffee product composed of coffee solids, combined and powdered with dextrina, maltose and dextrose added to protect the flavour.

98KA

ANOTHER OF NESTLÉ'S GOOD THINGS

Go on, spoil yourself. The origins of the firm of Fry's are way back in 1759, when a Quaker apothecary called Joseph Fry began making the drink of the day. That's what chocolate was then, a food in the form of a drink, often for breakfast, and Fry's bought

165

a Boulton & Watt steam engine with which to make it. Eventually it was discovered how to make chocolate you could eat, and Fry's Chocolate Cream in 1853 was one of the first wrapped bars made in large numbers.

Later, Fry's Five Boys had one boy's face on the wrapper pictured with the five expressions he would show while waiting for his square of milk chocolate. These expressions were named as: desperation, pacification, expectation, acclamation, realization (with a zed). We can only speculate on the discussions around the boardrooms, ad agencies and focus groups were anyone to suggest today using such long words on a children's chocolate bar. There was also Fry's Chocolate Sandwich, a bar of two thin layers of milk chocolate with a layer of dark between, which was the Double Milk version, or vice versa.

Most of us will be able to sing the tune of Fry's Turkish Delight, remembering that it was full of eastern promise, but we may not know that Fry's are said to have made the first chocolate Easter egg and were at one time the largest chocolate company in Britain and the biggest employer in Bristol.

Like so many pioneers, Fry's failed to keep up with the pace of innovation by late-coming rivals, in this case Quaker upstarts Cadbury and Rowntree. Fry's formed a joint company with Cadbury's in 1919 and became a subsidiary in 1935. Even before the Kraft takeover, Fry's production was being moved to Poland.

Not in my shop window. Yes, you might find Berlei and Gossard, brands that went via Courtauld to Sara Lee (Wonderbra and Playtex), to DBApparel and back to Courtauld again, but not Kayser Bondor. If you happen to be down Letchworth way, you could pass one very impressive Kayser Bondor factory that's now a Tesco. Another in Baldock was knocked down to make way for a housing estate.

Our ad is from 1943. The selling proposition, that the products were 'tailored', resulted later in the strangest couple of tailors ever seen in advertising, or anywhere else for that matter. Flying about the illustrated ladies, who lounged elegantly in their semi-diaphanous lingerie, were two tiny cupids dressed in black jacket (with wings sticking out) and pin-stripe trousers. Instead of the traditional bow and arrow, these little chaps wielded tape measures.

Kayser Underwear fits because it's tailored

KAYSER-BONDOR

.... and all Kayser-Bondor stockings are full-fashioned

Biscuits digested. Meredith & Drew, established 1830, in the 1880s were offering a Cyclist Biscuit 'for the road' that was 'highly nitrogenous and digestive'. Quite how and why cyclists should benefit from a biscuit high in nitrogen is not explained. Arrowroot, Abernethy, Captain, Butter, Plain and Ginger Brighton biscuits

M&D
Coronation Assortment

of sweet Biscuits including Cream Sandwiches, Chocolate Biscuits, Shortcakes, etc.

A wonderful assortment of biscuits, in a richness and variety not seen since the war. The full-colour souvenir tin makes a delightful permanent biscuit box and can be refilled with the famous 'M & D' "see-what-you-buy" pack.

4/3

In handsome souvenir 1 lb. tin

'M & D' BISCUITS ARE MADE BY MEREDITH & DREW LTD

were 'delivered in secured packets' and in secured tins. The factory was then in Shadwell, East London, where they also made the famous Dundee cake in two, four and six pound sizes, offered in 1901 at tenpence a pound. Later, there was a factory in Halifax.

A bid from Allied Bakeries was resisted in 1955 and the firm joined McVitie & Price, Macfarlane Lang and the rest in United Biscuits in 1967, to disappear without trace. Part of the Halifax factory is now a table tennis centre.

Cars in the high street. In the mid-1950s, cars were advertised as being able to start, being rainproof and having a heater. Even better if you could have a chrome surround to your rear window. They don't know they're born, these boy racers we have now.

Spacious ... Powerful ... Economical—That's Vauxhall Value!

Wyvern, £535, *plus* £268 17s. P.T.   Velox, £580, *plus* £291 7s. P.T.   Cresta, £640, £321 7s. P.T.

M^CNAMARA
MOTORS LIMITED

ST. HELEN'S STREET, IPSWICH   Telephone: 3775-6 and 3366

What you won't find at a grocer's, if you can find a grocer's. The name of Hayward's is still on jars of pickled onions and beetroot, and they're made still in the old factory at Bury St Edmunds, but by Premier Foods. Hayward Brothers was bought by Brooke Bond then by Premier, who no longer make Military Pickle and never did make its sibling Military Sauce, which disappeared long ago. Premier also no longer make PanYan, but they do make Branston and Sharwood's.

You can make your own approximation to Hayward's Military Pickle by chopping and mixing a pound (or 500 grams if you insist) each of cooking apple, block dates, dried vine fruit, onion and brown sugar with a short pint of malt vinegar, a good shake of salt, and a dessertspoon of curry powder. Use less sugar if you prefer, and more curry powder, and/or add some cayenne pepper. Bring to the boil, simmer for a few minutes and bottle.

Hammond's Yorkshire Relish Thick and Yorkshire Relish Thin, originally made by Goodall Backhouse of gravy browning fame, always superior in this correspondent's mind to HP and Lea & Perrins respectively, have also gone except, would you believe, in Ireland. Goodall's is a Premier Foods brand there and, if you're Irish, you can come into the parlour and see Goodall's Yorkshire Relish (thin) and YR Sauce (thick). Should you be unable to afford

172

Ballito silk stockings (see above) and therefore wish to colour your legs with Goodall's Gravy Browning, you will also have to go to Ireland because Premier prefers Bisto everywhere else.

Nothing blacks blacker. Advertising may have been full of nonsense in the old days, but at least you knew where you were with it. In present times, instead of a delight to maid and master that beats the world and self-polishes to a patent leather shine,

lasting a week on gents' boots and a month on ladies', you'd have some weasely rubbish like 'No blacking is more complete'.

What, no blue whitener? Omo is a river and region of Ethiopia, the Older Men's Organisation of Ireland, and a big washing name in Australia, Finland, Turkey, Switzerland, Holland and elsewhere, but not in the UK any more. When you could buy it here, it used to add brightness to whiteness.

Before that, it made things dazzling white. You only needed to boil; Omo bleacher, cleanser and purifier did the rest. Not for colours or woollens, you put the white things into cold water with Omo, brought to the boil in your wash-copper, let them boil for half an hour, rinsed and hung out to dry. No rubbing, no scrubbing. A threepenny packet yielded ten gallons of splendid washing fluid. On a Monday, naturally.

The brand name originated with Hudson's Soap. Robert Hudson was a Birmingham pharmacist who invented the first dry soap powder in 1837 and became very successful with it, building a large factory in Liverpool. He also developed a kind of washing-up liquid that he called Extract of Soap. The firm was taken over by Lever Brothers in 1908.

Into each life, some rain must fall. Rain was always welcome when you were working on the bingo on Scarborough sea front, or any other sea front, in the 1960s. In would come the happy holiday-makers, dripping and creaking with their Pakamacs quickly donned over their promenade wear. At this distance we have no way of knowing if they were genuine Pakamacs made by Servitor Plastic Products of Manchester. They didn't seem as substantial as the ones in this ad. They were more transparent, pinkish, or bluish. Anyway,

Pakamacs and Servitor have gone, but the name continues, in folklore and as a generic, like Hoover. It seems that Servitor was bought by Black & Edgington, which is now Arena Structures offering 'Total event solutions' but not Scarborough sea-front bingo rain solutions.

Bom-bom-bom-bom, Esso Blue. There were three main brands of paraffin: Regent Green, the least common; Esso Blue, advertised on television; and Aladdin Pink, made by Shell/BP, here advertised in

1956. There was absolutely no difference between them, despite the claim here that Pink is the best and most economical. Paraffin is a clear liquid, so all the makers did was add a colouring dye to render it saleable as a brand. Fire-eaters used to say that Aladdin Pink didn't taste quite as awful as Esso Blue, but that was the only known result of consumer tests.

When paraffin purity regulations were brought in by the EC, the green, pink and blue had to be taken out, so there was no selling proposition any more.

You'll wonder where the yellow went and, indeed, you may wonder where Pepsodent went. Our advert, from 1943, made the familiar claim (familiar to those of a certain age) that Pepsodent was unique in containing Irium, the super-cleanser that flushes film away. There is no such thing as irium, but there is sodium laurel sulphate, a surfactant used in all manner of cleaning agents such as degreasers, car washes, shampoos and toothpastes.

Well, you won't find Pepsodent in the UK now but you certainly will in India and Indonesia, where it's Unilever and big-big-big, and in North America where it's Church & Dwight and what we might call a basic or value brand, that is, cheaper than the rest and probably just as good. It is only soap, after all.

You could put a tiger in your tank once upon a time, and the Esso sign meant happy motoring. That's Shell, that was, and Fina gave you Superformance, unequalled by any other petrol. Here (pp. 179–80), in 1955, we have two entirely different approaches to the same problem: how do you persuade people that one petrol is better than another, when the people know that petrols are all the same? Well, not quite, because National Benzole was unique in having a spirit distilled from coal added to it, hence the academic approach to the advertisement, assuming we have half an hour spare to read all about it.

The boy-racer tactic, meanwhile, offered more energy for all cars and greater freedom from engine knock with BP Super, because it was platinum-processed, whatever that may have meant. The car featured, the Ford Zephyr, the middle one of the range – Consul, Zephyr, Zodiac – was a remarkable design for the time, paying a

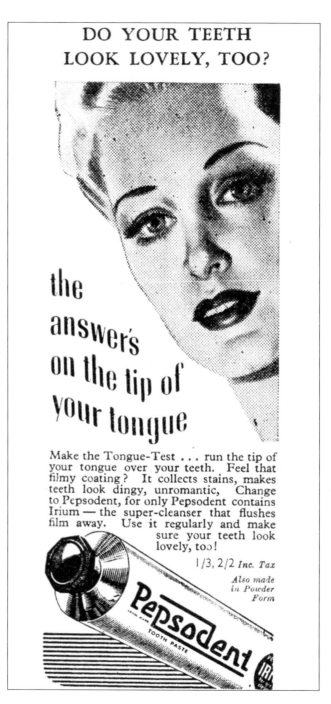

very restrained, British kind of homage to the new American styles which had boots sticking out at the back as big as their bonnets (or trunks as big as their hoods). Naturally, we stopped short of chromium-plated fins.

Success at Silverstone on new BP Super

In the Production Touring Car Race at the Daily Express Trophy meeting at Silverstone, Ken Wharton, using new BP Super in his Ford Zephyr, was placed first in the 2001 to 3000 c.c. class. Wharton's brilliant driving round the 25 laps of this 75 miles race showed what lively performance you can get from a car running on a super petrol. Because it is platinum-processed, new BP Super gives all cars more energy per gallon and greater freedom from engine-knock.

Knocking is a phenomenon virtually unknown today, but it was a real problem when fuels were not so good. The problem was largely solved by increasing the octane rating of petrol and adding a compound of lead, and later solved entirely in normal cars by modern engineering science. It still occurs in highly tuned engines and other manifestations of dissatisfaction with the motorist's average lot, but all drivers of a certain age will remember changing rapidly down as their engines made the dread sound due to their being at too low revs in too high a gear.

Before your very eyes. George Payne & Co. of Croydon made Lift instant lemon tea as well as Poppets and Just Brazils. Poppets were introduced in 1937, the idea developing from the installation of newfangled vending machines in cinema foyers. The toffee flavour Poppet in a small, handy box was followed swiftly by orange, mint, raisin, coconut, peanut and more.

As well as Arthur 'Oh what a glorious thing to be' Askey and his daughter Anthea, this ad from the 1950s deploys a couple of lines of deathless copywriting prose: *Centres to please every member of every family*, and *Caramels – Nuts – Creams – Etc.* They don't write 'em like that any more.

Payne's was bought by Northern Foods in 1998, which also bought Fox's, of Glacier Mint fame, in 2001 from Nestlé (not to be confused with Fox's Biscuits, also part of Northern Foods). The two confectionery companies were mingled but never really fitted in with the pork pies and the milk, and so Fox's mints and Payne's Poppets were sold off to a new company called Big Bear, he being the bear standing on the mint, formed especially to do this and to find other famous old brands that could be revitalised. At the time of writing, they have purchased from Pepsico the honey monster to go with the bear, in Sugar Puffs, and another old favourite, Quaker Puffed Wheat now without the Quaker. It's no longer shot from guns either, but then nothing's as good as it used to be.

Nice one, Cyril, and I'm the mother in Mother's Pride. There have been many attempts at branding bread, from Hovis to Mother's Pride to Nimble, Sunblest and Turog, and Procea was just that. It

was a leading brand, attractive enough to tempt James Goldsmith to take it into Cavenham Foods, when it was known as a slimming bread. After it was discovered that there is no such thing as a slimming bread, and that real bread is made from Iron Age grains such as emmer and spelt, and that real girls eat their crusts, Procea disappeared from our lives.

Hands that do dishes. Crosfield's was a very old soap-making and chemicals firm, bought by Brunner Mond in 1911, then by Lever Brothers and thence Unilever, then back to Mond in the shape of ICI in 1997, sold on again, and gone as a name. Meanwhile, as a subsidiary of Unilever, it made Quix washing-up liquid, the first detergent of its kind.

Younger readers will not be able to comprehend a world without such a thing, but we used to use pieces of soap in a small whisking basket, or soap powder, until Quix and Sqezy came along. The Sqezy bottle lived on as an expression long after the product was rendered invisible by Fairy Liquid, and Easy Peasy Lemon Sqezy remains a mantra used by many who have never seen the stuff. The brand was bought by Chartered Brands of Edinburgh from Unilever in 2000.

You can still get Quix in Chile, where the adverts do not feature Dan Dare offering to do the washing-up. And we didn't even know Dan Dare was married (next page).

Sturdy bones and strong white teeth. Those readers of a certain age to whom we so often refer, being of that age ourselves, will remember as children being plied with California Syrup of Figs, Virol, cod liver oil (in capsules if we were lucky – remember how it used to repeat?), Iron Jelloids and Scott's Emulsion. Parents born in the first few decades of the twentieth century had parents who knew all about infant mortality, rickets, malnutrition and the other afflictions that beset the mass of people so, although post-WWII children in Britain had little to fear from much of this, the trace memory was there. The fig, the malt of the barley and the codfish would ensure our survival and healthy growth.

The advertising copy that follows is from late nineteenth-century America, a time and a place where no restrictions were placed on

advertising, in the sense of factual accuracy or, for that matter, good taste, and no medicine-seller had to prove that his snake oil did what it said on the bottle:

Unfortunately in every household some of the little ones are the victims of a wasting disorder. For some reason their food fails to nourish them, and they finally fade and die. We are glad that we have a food and remedy of unequalled potency in all conditions of wasting, of whatever character, in children as well as in adults. SCOTT'S EMULSION OF COD LIVER OIL WITH THE HYPO-PHOSPHITES OF LIME AND SODA is really a marvelous remedy in producing flesh and strength. It is surprising how quickly it checks the waste and decline in flesh. It is so prepared that the most sickly child can digest and assimilate it readily, even when the stomach will not tolerate ordinary food. In addition to its great flesh-producing and strengthening powers IT IS THE BEST REMEDY IN EXISTENCE for Consumption, Scrofula, Colds and Chronic Coughs, Anaemia and General Debility. It heals the irritation of the lungs and throat, cures the cough, and gives strength in a manner surprising both to physician and patient. For ordinary Colds and Coughs no specific or cough remedy equals it. It not only cures the cold at once, but builds up and strengthens the system. IT IS ALMOST AS PALATABLE AS MILK. Do not fail to try this invaluable remedy for any condition of wasting, either in children or adults.

The manufacturers today of Scott's Emulsion, GlaxoSmithKline, do not claim to be able to stop your child from dying, but only that 'The *Scott's* brand is a cod liver oil range of emulsions rich in natural sources of vitamin A and D, calcium, phosphorus and omega 3. The emulsion helps build up the body's natural resistance to infections and develop strong bones and teeth.' The product is available in many countries, such as Mexico, Malaysia and Pakistan.

Too much of a good thing can result in overdosing on Vitamin A, a nasty condition of which the symptoms range from nausea to cessation of existence. You can get this by eating a polar bear's liver, presumably because polar bears eat seals which eat nothing but fish, or a walrus's liver. So beware, next time you go on an Arctic exploration. The liver of the husky is not so good either.

Happy as the day is long—

are the little ones who are strengthened & nourished by this body-building food. Ask for

Scott's Emulsion

Each spoonful leads to Health—

It protects the throat and lungs and gives strength to resist weakness & disease.

TRADE MARK

They used to make cod liver oil by filling a barrel with livers – how many cod's livers does it take to fill a barrel? No wonder the stocks of cod have collapsed – and topping it up with sea water. You then waited until the oil separated out, which could take months. Modern methods use rather more of the fish.

Children's shoes have far to go. In 1952, the everyday story of country folk had been running for a year, and Mrs Dale had been rather worried about Jim for four years. They were national institutions, like the shoe industry.

Every high street used to have several shoe shops. Mostly, those shoe chains began in the days of the boot, well before the First World War, when fashion in footwear, or any variation in design and materials, was entirely the province of those who could afford hand-made, bespoke shoes from the finest craftsmen and, possibly more important, could also afford to be taken everywhere by carriage and cabriolet. The rest of us wore heavy boots or clogs and walked, along muddy roads thick with horse manure. We were very glad when someone opened a shop selling these essentials cheaply, and doubly glad when public transport developed to such an extent, in the big cities at any rate, that we could indulge ourselves in lighter, smarter footwear.

Of course, the factories and shop chains were equally adept at supplying these new styles as they had been with the old daisy roots, but it took a while for the retailing and manufacturing sides of the industry to get into sync with trends in fashion, as business picked up after the Great War. Ladies' shoes especially were subject to the shifting mists of fashion trends. Shoe shops were often left with large quantities of stock which had been just the very thing yesterday but today, alas, were just too, too passé. The dust settled by about 1925 and previously unimagined materials began to be used, like python skins, ostrich skins, shark, lizard and so on.

In 1924, the British shoe industry made almost 120 million pairs of shoes, boots and slippers, about 85 per cent of which were sold in the home countries, which works out at slightly more than two pairs for every man, woman and child. So who was supplying this huge market, and what happened to them?

Dolcis was started by John Upson in 1863 from a barrow in Woolwich. The company floated on the Stock Exchange in 1920, became part of the British Shoe Corporation in 1956, Alexon Group in 1998, was bought by John Kinnaird in 2007, went bust in 2008. At that time, Dolcis had 1,200 employees and 185 stores and concessions; 600 staff lost their jobs there and then, and eighty-nine

Norman Painting, Gwen Berryman, Pamela Mant and Harry Oakes who play the parts of 'The Archers' in the popular B.B.C. Serial.

'The Archers' choose

Spire and White Queen

shoes

The 'Archer' family all find shoes to suit them in the Spire and White Queen ranges. The men appreciate the sturdy build and fine leathers of the many Spire styles, whilst the ladies like White Queen for their clever combination of fashion and comfort. For the children there are 'Junior' shoes in each range.

See the wide range of

Shoes for the whole family

at your local stockists at prices to suit all

Spire	White Queen	Juniors
47/6 to 75/-	39/11 to 55/-	15/- to 42/-

G. T. WHITE SHOE CO. LTD. LEICESTER

stores were closed. The name and stock for some stores were bought by Stylo and the rest were put up for sale.

George Clark, a man with a small shoemaking firm in Kilmarnock, and two brothers called Abbott, had the idea of making men's boots and shoes in different widths, a novelty then. They formed Saxone in 1901. They joined with Lilley & Skinner in 1957. By 1960, there were 170 shops and two factories.

William Timpson was an apprentice bootmaker in Northampton but decided to go into retailing instead. He opened his first shop in Manchester when he was 16 years old, in 1865, and another in 1869. Cautiously he expanded, and built a small factory. The business really took off in the 1930s, opening ten shops a year. By the start of the Second World War there were 189 shops, mainly in the north of England and Scotland, plus eleven factories making 17,000 pairs a week. The firm was bought by United Drapery Stores (John Collier, basically) in 1972, which was bought by Hanson Trust in 1983, followed by a Timpson family buy-out later the same year. The family sold all their shoe shops in 1987 and are now key-cutting, locksmithing, shoe repairing, making signs and trophies and more, in 600 different family-owned shops.

Stead & Simpson, owners of Shoe Express, Lilley & Skinner and Peter Briggs, in 2008 went into administration, which left large numbers of shoe-makers gasping for air and money. Shoe Zone bought S&S and took over 300 stores from the 375 chain, meaning that perhaps only 500 out of 3,000 jobs were lost.

Most of the other names we knew – Freeman, Hardy & Willis, for example – ended up in Sir Charles Clore's British Shoe Corporation and, by various routes from there, went bust and disappeared. In Leicestershire, mostly, a vast network of shoe factories had been set up, by such firms and by more who just manufactured, to meet what seemed to be an insatiable demand for footwear made of leather and, to an extent, footwear made of artificial materials but in the style of leather.

These factories were very good at what they did, very efficient, and there seemed no end to the public's habit of buying shoes on the high street like they had done for a century. Even Sir Charles Clore couldn't see an end to it, or he wouldn't have bought 3,000 shoe shops. Then Marks & Spencer started selling shoes, and big mail order stores, and the supermarkets and then, in a very short time indeed, something quite extraordinary happened. Half the world took to plimsolls.

Those gym shoes we wore at school, for the cross-country and the 220 yards and playing pirates, had been redesigned and rebranded. Instead of being something rather smelly in a kit bag at the squash club, sports shoes, trainers as they were suddenly called, became everyday wear, everywhere. People removed their shoes and put on trainers instead. The new Saxone was JJB Sports. The new Freeman, Hardy & Willis was Reebok at Sports Direct. And nobody in the shoe trade had seen it coming.

Van Heusen was a big name in shirts for most of the twentieth century and still is, of course, as part of the Phillips Van Heusen group that also owns Calvin Klein and Tommy Hilfiger. The firm began in nineteenth-century America, making shirts by hand for coalminers. By the 1920s they had patented the self-folding collar and introduced collar-attached shirts.

Vantella as a brand name was in use in the 1930s, and here in our ad in the 1960s, but probably didn't suit the male fashion market

Add Tone to Good Tailoring

A Vantella Shirt invariably sets off a man's appearance to better advantage; for it has a crisp quality and easy comfort entirely appropriate to good cloth, and well-cut clothes.

VANTELLA Regd.
SHIRTS
feature the exclusive
VAN HEUSEN
woven-on-a-curve Collars to match and to spare and replaceable Cuffs and Neckbands. Very few shirts indeed look so well, last so long, or, in their excellence, cost so little.

Obtainable at leading Outfitters everywhere in really smart patterns—and in white—at the reduced price of 49/6d.

Fully illustrated Pattern Cards are obtainable from
ADVERTISEMENT MANAGER
VANTELLA · 465 OXFORD ST. · LONDON · W.1
SHOP EARLY AND AVOID THE CHRISTMAS RUSH FOR VANTELLA

of more modern times. Still, there's something vaguely pleasant about being persuaded to buy a shirt with words like 'Very few shirts indeed look so well, last so long or, in their excellence, cost so little'. Can you see that on an ad for Calvin Klein underpants?

What you won't find at a tobacconist, if you could find a tobacconist. Balkan Sobranie, like Baby's Bottom and almost all pipe smokers, has gone. Legislated and politically corrected out of existence, it has vanished, with the result that it is now much, much simpler to buy marijuana than pipe tobacco, and much, much simpler to take cocaine, and to find somewhere to take it, than it is to smoke a pipe of Balkan Sobranie or, indeed, to find somewhere you might have a chance of catching the unmistakeable aroma (next page).

What you won't find at a tobacconist, if you could find a tobacconist. Churchman's Number One (page 193) was first made in Portman Road, Ipswich in 1896, when the old London tobacco firm of W A & A C Churchman bought a cigarette-rolling machine, one of the first in the country, and installed it in their new factory there. This machine could make 10,000 fags an hour.

In 1901, in response to aggressive noises from American Tobacco, W D & H O Wills, John Player and others formed Imperial Tobacco; Churchman joined up in 1902. After that, apart from battles between brands, nothing really disturbed the cigarette industry for many years. Everybody smoked away like mad in pubs, cinemas, theatres, restaurants, the workplace unless it was a firework factory, and at home. Then came the link with lung cancer, proved in the 1950s after being suspected since 1929, and the fag companies were suddenly on the retreat.

Big fat untipped brands like Churchman's, Senior Service, Player's, State Express, Capstan and so on were especially hard hit and not all of them could be kept going. Churchman's in the 1950s had been considered worth a long-running advertising campaign featuring illustrations of attractive females asking for a smoke with the words 'Darling, do give me a Churchman's No 1'. Later there were ads featuring pheasants that were safe for fifteen minutes while the shootist had his ciggy and, even more bizarre, horses and dogs that smoked and told their human partners to hang around

LIGHT UP AND PIPE DOWN

Your favourite briar with Balkan Sobranie glowing in the bowl is the perfect answer to present discontents, a quiet smoke your refuge from a raucous world, and Balkan Sobranie is your best contribution to noisy debate. So light up, and, in your wisdom, pipe down . . . The exciting Balkan Sobranie Virginian No. 10 adds to the best Virginia a touch of the leaf that has made certain cigars world famous — the touch of Sobranie genius. It gives you a long satisfying smoke and an aroma of which even the ladies approve.

Price: 5/9 per oz; 11/6 for 2 ozs.

VIRGINIAN No. 10

SOBRANIE LTD. 136 CITY ROAD LONDON E.C.1

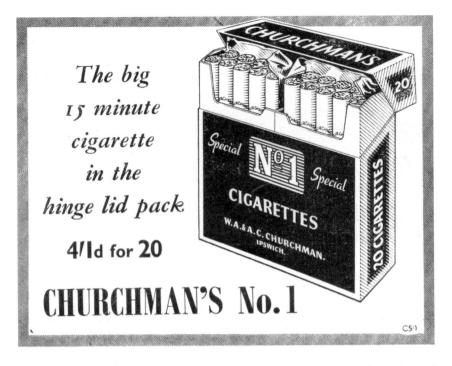

The big
15 minute
cigarette
in the
hinge lid pack

4/1d for 20

CHURCHMAN'S No.1

for fifteen minutes. No such efforts were made later and the brand fell victim to its own boast. It was cut out as a name in 1972 and the factory was closed in 1992, putting 400 people out of work.

De Reske Minors, a small, Woodbine/Park Drive type, used to advertise in wartime as the 'Ten Minute Smoke for all Service folk', twenty for 10d then, fifteen for two shillings in 1953 when Churchman's No 1, 'the fifteen-minute smoke', were 3/9 for twenty. Taking an average between rises in earnings and prices since then, we're talking eight quid a packet.

Cars in the High Street. Wolseleys were always that little bit upmarket, like Rovers used to be, aimed directly at the British middle class. Over the page we have a chap who owns horses and spaniels, going off to war in 1943. He's obviously a major at least and more likely a colonel, because he has a moustache, a wife he calls Susan, and he says things like 'D'you know'.

Nobody by the name of Wolseley ever had anything to do with the cars. It was Herbert Austin, works manager of the Wolseley

A soldier's farewell to his Wolseley

MY leave is up tomorrow . . . I'm wondering if Susan will give the spaniels enough exercise and cherish my Wolseley. D'you know, I'm terribly attached to that car. Wolseleys are beautifully made and have that sort of thorough, honest workmanship so characteristic of the British way of doing things. It is something the world cannot and will not do without.

WOLSELEY

—made by **NUFFIELD**—a name you can trust

Announcement of THE NUFFIELD ORGANIZATION
— a cornerstone of Britain's Industrial Structure

Sheep Shearing Machine Co. who started making the cars, and he left to set up his own firm which became quite well known. Even so, by the mid 1920s, Wolseley was the biggest British car manufacturer, whereupon it went bust and was bought up by Morris. After the Second World War, featuring our colonel, Wolseley cars became little more than slightly adapted, more luxurious and rebadged versions of general designs for the Nuffield group, then British Motor Corporation, then British Leyland. The last car with the Wolseley name was made in 1975.

Few items of shopping are as symbolic of the difference between then and now as boys' shorts. Tracksuits? Never heard of them. Trainers? What are they? Flannel shorts, with long woollen stockings and lace-up leather shoes? Now you're talking. With pockets set forward to reduce strain. The strain, however, proved too much for Uwin and Douglas Warne, long gone.

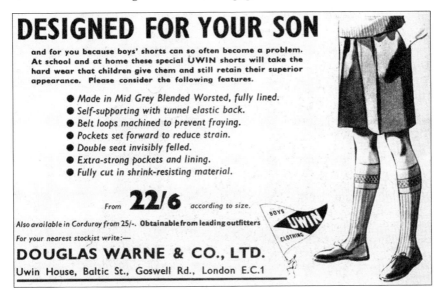

DESIGNED FOR YOUR SON

and for you because boys' shorts can so often become a problem. At school and at home these special UWIN shorts will take the hard wear that children give them and still retain their superior appearance. Please consider the following features.

- Made in Mid Grey Blended Worsted, fully lined.
- Self-supporting with tunnel elastic back.
- Belt loops machined to prevent fraying.
- Pockets set forward to reduce strain.
- Double seat invisibly felled.
- Extra-strong pockets and lining.
- Fully cut in shrink-resisting material.

From **22/6** according to size.

Also available in Corduroy from 25/-. Obtainable from leading outfitters

For your nearest stockist write:—

DOUGLAS WARNE & CO., LTD.

Uwin House, Baltic St., Goswell Rd., London E.C.1

One of the oldest biscuit firms, Wright's began in 1791 as L Wright & Son. In the twentieth century, the face of the company was a character called Mischief, a small boy who had a sister called Marie. South Shields (For Happy Seaside Outings), at the mouth

of the Tyne, otherwise known for shipbuilding (now gone) and coalmining (now gone) was also known for Wright's Biscuits with that brilliant trademark of the little horror. He finally disappeared in 1973 when the factory closed.

And so we must take our leave of the high street. It's been a pleasant stroll, down memory lane as it were, and one that is becoming more and more difficult to do in real life. We must admit that the globe-wide range and the average quality of goods in supermarkets are far greater than ever was the case on any high street, and it's a lot easier to choose and order something on the internet than it is to trog down the road to get it.

Apparently, the high pace and the cosmopolitan, educated tastes of modern life demand such convenience and variety as were undreamed of in times not that long ago. Still, as the jar of cook-in sauce said to the bag of salad, I think we might be missing something.

Long, long before photographers could be arrested as suspected terrorists, anyone with a camera could still get a funny look from the constabulary, as here, in Morden, sometime around 1950.

Perth in the 1960s. Your correspondent remembers wandering aimlessly up and down this street with some friends, waiting for the pubs to open. We'd had a few days on the Cuillins in Skye and our departure was not until 10 pm, on the motorail sleeper to Olympia. So that's two things you couldn't do today. The pubs are open in the afternoon, and there's no motorail in Britain any more.

Doncaster, late 1940s or early 1950s, well before the bypass anyway, had the Great North Road as its high street, as did many other towns, such as Biggleswade, Baldock, Boroughbridge, Stamford, Newark and Bawtry. Sunshine, everyone in a hat, trolley-bus wires – memories are made of this.

Greengate Street in Stafford, 1948 or thereabouts, has none of the really big chains showing, not in this picture at any rate. They'll be there, somewhere, of course, but such variety of local shops will never be seen again.

Index

Smith 123
Tetley 131
Uwin 195
Van Heusen 190
Wall 140

Whiteley 143
Wolseley 193
Woolworth 148
Wright 195